PYTHON ONE-LINERS

PYTHON ONE-LINERS

Write Concise, Eloquent Python Like a Professional

by Christian Mayer

no starch press

San Francisco

Printed in USA

First printing

24 23 22 21 20   1 2 3 4 5 6 7 8 9

ISBN-10: 1-7185-0050-5
ISBN-13: 978-1-7185-0050-1

Publisher: William Pollock
Production Editors: Janelle Ludowise and Kassie Andreadis
Cover Illustration: Rob Gale
Interior Design: Octopod Studios
Developmental Editors: Liz Chadwick and Alex Freed
Technical Reviewer: Daniel Zingaro
Copyeditor: Sharon Wilkey
Compositor: Danielle Foster
Proofreader: James Fraleigh
Indexer: JoAnne Burek

For information on distribution, translations, or bulk sales, please contact No Starch Press, Inc. directly:
No Starch Press, Inc.
245 8th Street, San Francisco, CA 94103
phone: 1.415.863.9900; info@nostarch.com
www.nostarch.com

The Library of Congress issued the following Cataloging-in-Publication Data for the first edition:

```
Names: Mayer, Christian (Computer Scientist), author.
Title: Python one-liners: write concise, eloquent Python like a professional / Christian Mayer.
Description: San Francisco : No Starch Press, Inc., 2020. | Includes index.
Identifiers: LCCN 2020001449 (print) | LCCN 2020001450 (ebook) | ISBN
   9781718500501 | ISBN 9781718500518 (ebook)
Subjects: LCSH: Python (Computer program language)
Classification: LCC QA76.73.P98 M39 2020  (print) | LCC QA76.73.P98
   (ebook) | DDC 005.13/3--dc23
LC record available at https://lccn.loc.gov/2020001449
LC ebook record available at https://lccn.loc.gov/2020001450
```

To my wife Anna

About the Author

Christian Mayer is a doctor of computer science and the founder and maintainer of the popular Python site *https://blog.finxter.com/* and its associated newsletter, which has 20,000 active subscribers and is still growing. His rapidly growing websites help tens of thousands of students improve their coding skills and online businesses. Christian is also the author of the *Coffee Break Python* series of self-published books.

About the Technical Reviewer

Dr. Daniel Zingaro is an assistant teaching professor of computer science and award-winning teacher at the University of Toronto. His main area of research is computer science education, where he studies how students learn (and sometimes don't learn) computer science material. He is the author of *Algorithmic Thinking* (forthcoming from No Starch Press).

BRIEF CONTENTS

CONTENTS IN DETAIL

6
ALGORITHMS   151

ACKNOWLEDGMENTS

The world doesn't need more books; it needs better books. I'm incredibly grateful to the people at No Starch Press for putting everything at work toward this philosophy. This book is the result of their invaluable advice, constructive feedback, and hundreds of hours of diligent work. My deep gratitude goes to the No Starch team for making the book-writing process such a fun experience.

In particular, I'd like to thank Bill Pollock for inviting me to write this book and for providing me inspiration and deep insights into the publishing world.

I'm very grateful for my brilliant content editor, Liz Chadwick, who skillfully, patiently, and eloquently transformed my rough drafts into a much more human-readable form. It's because of her excellent support that the book reached a level of clarity I would have never imagined when starting this project.

I want to express my appreciation to Alex Freed for her relentless focus on improving the text quality. It has been an honor to work together with such a talented editor.

I'd like to thank my production editor, Janelle Ludowise, for polishing the book with a great love for every detail. Janelle put her skills to work—in a positive and enthusiastic manner—to craft the final version of the book.

Thanks, Janelle. Many thanks as well to Kassie Andreadis, who energetically pushed the book through to completion.

My distinctive appreciation goes to Professor Daniel Zingaro. He didn't shy away from investing much of his time, effort, and excellent computer science skills into eradicating inaccuracies from the book. He also contributed many wonderful suggestions that brought clarity to the book. Without his effort, the book would not only contain more bugs but also be harder to read. That said, any inaccuracies that remain are my own.

My doctorate supervisor, Professor Rothermel, contributed indirectly to this book by investing considerable time, skill, and effort into my computer science education. I owe him my deepest gratitude and appreciation.

I'm forever grateful to my beautiful wife, Anna Altimira, who keeps listening to, encouraging, and supporting even my wildest ideas. I'm also thankful to my kids, Amalie and Gabriel, for their inspiring curiosity and the happiness they bring to my life through thousands of smiles.

Lastly, the greatest source of motivation came from the active members of the Finxter community. First and foremost, I've written this book for ambitious coders—like you—who want to advance their coding skills and solve practical problems in the real world. After long working days, it was grateful emails from Finxter members that encouraged me to write more sections of the book.

INTRODUCTION

With this book, I want to help you become
a Python expert. To do this, we're going
to focus on *Python one-liners*: concise, useful
programs packed into a single line of Python.
Focusing on one-liners will help you read and write
code faster and more concisely, and will improve your
understanding of the language.

There are five more reasons I think learning Python one-liners will
help you improve and are worth studying.

First, by improving your core Python skills, you'll be able to overcome
many of the small programming weaknesses that hold you back. It's hard to
make progress without a profound understanding of the basics. Single lines
of code are the basic building block of any program. Understanding these
basic building blocks will help you master high-level complexity without
feeling overwhelmed.

Second, you'll learn how to leverage wildly popular Python libraries,
such as those for data science and machine learning. The book consists of

five one-liner chapters, each addressing a different area of Python, from regular expressions to machine learning. This approach will give you an overview of possible Python applications you can build, as well as teach you how to use these powerful libraries.

Third, you'll learn to write more Pythonic code. Python beginners, especially those coming from other programming languages, often write code in un-Pythonic ways. We'll cover Python-specific concepts like list comprehension, multiple assignment, and slicing, all of which will help you write code that's easily readable and sharable with other programmers in the field.

Fourth, studying Python one-liners forces you to think clearly and concisely. When you're making every single code symbol count, there's no room for sparse and unfocused coding.

Fifth, your new one-liner skill set will allow you to see through overly complicated Python codebases, and impress friends and interviewers alike. You may also find it fun and satisfying to solve challenging programming problems with a single line of code. And you wouldn't be alone: a vibrant online community of Python geeks compete for the most compressed, most Pythonic solutions to various practical (and not-so-practical) problems.

Python One-Liner Example

The central thesis of this book is that learning Python one-liners is both fundamental to understanding more-advanced codebases and an excellent tool for improving your skills. Before understanding what's going on in a codebase with thousands of lines, you must understand the meaning of a single line of code.

Let's have a quick look at a Python one-liner. Don't worry if you don't fully understand it. You will master this one-liner in Chapter 6.

```
q = lambda l: q( ❶[x for x in l[1:] if x <= l[0]]) + [l[0]] + q([x for x in l if x > l[0]]) if l else []
```

This one-liner is a beautiful and concise way of compressing the famous Quicksort algorithm, though the meaning may be difficult to grasp for many Python beginners and intermediates.

Python one-liners often build on each other, so one-liners will increase in complexity throughout the book. In this book, we'll start with simple one-liners that will become the basis for more-complex one-liners later. For example, the preceding Quicksort one-liner is difficult and long, based on the easier concept of list comprehension ❶. Here's a simpler list comprehension that creates a list of squared numbers:

```
lst  = [x**2 for x in range(10)]
```

We can break this one-liner into even simpler one-liners that teach important Python basics, such as variable assignments, math operators, data structures, for loops, membership operators, and the range() function—all of which happens in a single line of Python!

Know that *basic* doesn't mean *trivial.* All the one-liners we'll look at are useful, and each chapter addresses a separate area or discipline in computer science, giving you a broad perspective on the power of Python.

A Note on Readability

The Zen of Python comprises 19 guiding principles for the Python programming languages. You can read it in your Python shell by entering import this:

```
>>> import this
The Zen of Python, by Tim Peters

Beautiful is better than ugly.
Explicit is better than implicit.
Simple is better than complex.
Complex is better than complicated.
Flat is better than nested.
Sparse is better than dense.
Readability counts.
--snip--
```

According to *The Zen of Python,* "Readability counts." One-liners are minimalistic programs to solve problems. In many cases, rewriting a piece of code as a Python one-liner will improve readability and make the code more Pythonic. An example is using *list comprehension* to reduce the creation of lists into a single line of code. Have a look at the following example:

```
# BEFORE
squares = []

for i in range(10):
    squares.append(i**2)

print(squares)
# [0, 1, 4, 9, 16, 25, 36, 49, 64, 81]
```

In this code snippet, we need five lines of code to create a list of the first 10 square numbers and print it to the shell. However, it's much better to use a one-liner solution that accomplishes the same thing in a more readable and concise way:

```
# AFTER
print([i**2 for i in range(10)])
# [0, 1, 4, 9, 16, 25, 36, 49, 64, 81]
```

The output is the same, but the one-liner builds on the more Pythonic concept of list comprehension. It's easier to read and more concise.

However, Python one-liners can also be hard to understand. In some cases, writing a solution as a Python one-liner isn't more readable. But just as the chess master must know all possible moves before deciding which one is best, you must know all ways of expressing your thoughts in code so that you can decide on the best one. Going for *the most beautiful* solution is not a low-priority matter; it's at the core of the Python ecosystem. As *The Zen of Python* teaches, "Beautiful is better than ugly."

Who Is This Book For?

Are you a beginner- to intermediate-level Python coder? Like many of your peers, you may be stuck in your coding progress. This book can help you out. You've read a lot of programming tutorials online. You've written your own source code and successfully shipped small projects. You've finished a basic programming course and read a programming textbook or two. Maybe you've even finished a technical program in college, where you've learned about the basics of computer science and programming.

Perhaps you're limited by certain beliefs, like that most coders understand source code much faster than you, or that you're nowhere near the top 10 percent of programmers. If you want to reach an advanced coding level and join the top coding experts, you need to learn new applicable skills.

I can relate because when I started out studying computer science 10 years ago, I struggled with the belief that I knew nothing about coding. At the same time, it seemed that all my peers were already very experienced and proficient.

In this book, I want to help you overcome these limiting beliefs and push you one step further toward Python mastery.

What Will You Learn?

Here is an overview of what you will learn.

Chapter 1: Python Refresher Introduces the very basics of Python to refresh your knowledge.

Chapter 2: Python Tricks Contains 10 one-liner tricks to help you master the basics, such as list comprehension, file input, the functions `lambda`, `map()`, and `zip()`, the `all()` quantifier, slicing, and basic list arithmetic. You'll also learn how to use, manipulate, and leverage data structures to solve various day-to-day problems.

Chapter 3: Data Science Contains 10 one-liners for data science, building on the NumPy library. NumPy is at the heart of Python's powerful machine learning and data science capabilities. You'll learn elementary NumPy basics such as array, shape, axis, type, broadcasting, advanced indexing, slicing, sorting, searching, aggregating, and statistics.

Chapter 4: Machine Learning Covers 10 one-liners for machine learning with Python's scikit-learn library. You'll learn about regression algorithms that predict values. Examples of these include linear regression, K-Nearest Neighbors, and neural networks. You'll also learn classification algorithms such as logistic regression, decision-tree learning, support-vector machines, and random forests. Furthermore, you'll learn about how to calculate basic statistics of multidimensional data arrays, and the K-Means algorithm for unsupervised learning. These algorithms and methods are among the most important algorithms in the field of machine learning.

Chapter 5: Regular Expressions   Contains 10 one-liners to help you achieve more with regular expressions. You'll learn about various basic regular expressions that you can combine (and recombine) in order to create more-advanced regular expressions, using grouping and named groups, negative lookaheads, escaped characters, whitespaces, character sets (and negative characters sets), and greedy/nongreedy operators.

Chapter 6: Algorithms   Contains 10 one-liner algorithms addressing a wide range of computer science topics, including anagrams, palindromes, supersets, permutations, factorials, prime numbers, Fibonacci numbers, obfuscation, searching, and algorithmic sorting. Many of these form the basis of more-advanced algorithms and contain the seeds of a thorough algorithmic education.

Afterword   Concludes this book and releases you into the real world, packed with your new and improved Python coding skills.

Online Resources

To enhance the training material in this book, I've added supplementary resources that you can find online at *https://pythononeliners.com/* or *http://www .nostarch.com/pythononeliners/*. The interactive resources include the following:

Python cheat sheets   You can download those Python cheat sheets as printable PDFs and pin them to your wall. The cheat sheets contain essential Python language features, and if you study them thoroughly, you can refresh your Python skills and ensure that you've closed any knowledge gap you may have.

One-liner video lessons   As part of my Python email course, I've recorded many Python one-liner lessons from this book, which you can access for free. Those lessons can assist you in your learning and provide a multimedia learning experience.

Python puzzles   You can visit the online resources to solve Python puzzles and use the *Finxter.com* app for free to test and train your Python skills and measure your learning progress as you go through the book.

Code files and Jupyter notebooks   You must roll up your sleeves and start working with code to make progress toward Python mastery. Take your time to play around with various parameter values and input data. For your convenience, I've added all Python one-liners as executable code files.

1

PYTHON REFRESHER

The purpose of this chapter is to refresh your knowledge of basic Python data structures, keywords, control flow operations, and other fundamentals. I wrote this book for intermediate Python programmers who want to reach the next level of programming expertise. To get to the expert level, you need a thorough study of the basics.

Understanding the basics allows you to take a step back and see the bigger picture—an important skill whether you want to become tech lead at Google, a computer science professor, or just a great programmer. For instance, computer science professors will often have an incredibly profound knowledge of the basics in their field that allows them to argue from first principles and identify research gaps, rather than being blinded by the latest state-of-the-art technology. This chapter presents the most important Python basics, which serve as a foundation for the more advanced topics in this book.

Basic Data Structures

A thorough understanding of data structures is one of the most fundamental skills you can acquire as a programmer. It will help you no matter whether you create machine learning projects, work on large code bases, set up and manage websites, or write algorithms.

Numerical Data Types and Structures

The two most important numerical data types are the integer and float. An *integer* is a positive or negative number without a floating point (for example, 3). A *float* is a positive or negative number with floating-point precision (for example, 3.14159265359). Python offers a wide variety of built-in numerical operations, as well as functionality to convert between those numerical data types. Study the examples in Listing 1-1 carefully to master these highly important numerical operations.

```
## Arithmetic Operations
x, y = 3, 2
print(x + y) # = 5
print(x - y) # = 1
print(x * y) # = 6
print(x / y) # = 1.5
print(x // y) # = 1
print(x % y) # = 1
print(-x) # = -3
print(abs(-x)) # = 3
print(int(3.9)) # = 3
print(float(x)) # = 3.0
print(x ** y) # = 9
```

Listing 1-1: The numerical data types

Most of the operators are self-explanatory. Note that the // operator performs integer division. The result is an integer value that is rounded down (for example, 3 // 2 == 1).

Booleans

A variable of type *Boolean* can take only two values—either False or True.

In Python, Boolean and integer data types are closely related: the Boolean data type internally uses integer values (by default, the Boolean value False is represented by integer 0, and the Boolean value True is represented by integer 1). Listing 1-2 gives an example of these two Boolean keywords.

```
x = 1 > 2
print(x)
# False

y = 2 > 1
```

```
print(y)
# True
```

Listing 1-2: The Boolean values False and True

After evaluating the given expressions, variable x refers to the Boolean value False, and variable y refers to the Boolean value True.

You can use Booleans with three important keywords to create more-complicated expressions in Python.

Keywords: and, or, not

Boolean expressions represent basic logical operators. Using them in combination with only the following three keywords, you can craft a wide variety of potentially complicated expressions:

and   The expression x and y evaluates to True if value x is True *and* value y is True. If either of those is False, the overall expression becomes False too.

or   The expression x or y evaluates to True if value x is True *or* value y is True (or both values are True). If even just one of those is True, the overall expression becomes True too.

not   The expression not x evaluates to True if value x is False. Otherwise, the expression evaluates to False.

Consider the following Python code in Listing 1-3.

```
x, y = True, False

print((x or y) == True)
# True

print((x and y) == False)
# True

print((not y) == True)
# True
```

Listing 1-3: The keywords and, or, and not

By using these three keywords, you can express all the logical expressions you'll ever need.

Boolean Operator Precedence

The order that Boolean operators are applied is an important aspect of understanding Boolean logic. For example, consider the natural language statement "it rains and it's cold or windy". We can interpret this in two ways:

"(it rains and it's cold) or windy"   In this case, the statement would be True if it is windy—even if it doesn't rain.

"it rains and (it's cold or windy)"   In this case, however, the statement would be False if it doesn't rain—no matter whether it's cold or windy.

The order of Boolean operators matters. The correct interpretation of this statement would be the first one because the and operator takes precedence before the or operator. Let's consider the code snippet in Listing 1-4.

```
## 1. Boolean Operations
x, y = True, False

print(x and not y)
# True

print(not x and y or x)
# True

## 2. If condition evaluates to False
if None or 0 or 0.0 or '' or [] or {} or set():
    print("Dead code") # Not reached
```

Listing 1-4: The Boolean data type

This code shows two important points. First, Boolean operators are ordered by priority—the operator not has the highest priority, followed by the operator and, followed by the operator or. Second, the following values are automatically evaluated to False: the keyword None, the integer value 0, the float value 0.0, empty strings, or empty container types.

Strings

Python *strings* are sequences of characters. Strings are immutable and so cannot be changed after creation. While other ways to create strings exist, these are the five most commonly used:

Single quotes   'Yes'

Double quotes   "Yes"

Triple quotes for multiline strings   '''Yes''' or """Yes"""

The string method   str(5) == '5' is True

Concatenation   'Py' + 'thon' becomes 'Python'

Often, you'll explicitly want to use *whitespace characters* in strings. The most frequently used whitespace characters are the newline character \n, the space character \s, and the tab character \t.

Listing 1-5 shows the most important string methods.

```
## Most Important String Methods
y = "   This is lazy\t\n   "

print(y.strip())
# Remove Whitespace: 'This is lazy'

print("DrDre".lower())
# Lowercase: 'drdre'
```

```
print("attention".upper())
# Uppercase: 'ATTENTION'

print("smartphone".startswith("smart"))
# Matches the string's prefix against the argument: True

print("smartphone".endswith("phone"))
# Matches the string's suffix against the argument: True

print("another".find("other"))
# Match index: 2

print("cheat".replace("ch", "m"))
# Replaces all occurrences of the first by the second argument: meat

print(','.join(["F", "B", "I"]))
# Glues together all elements in the list using the separator string: F,B,I

print(len("Rumpelstiltskin"))
# String length: 15

print("ear" in "earth")
# Contains: True
```

Listing 1-5: The string data type

This non-exclusive list of string methods shows that the string data type is powerful, and you can solve many common string problems with built-in Python functionality. If in doubt about how to achieve a certain result regarding string problems, consult the online reference listing all built-in string methods: *https://docs.python.org/3/library/string.html#module-string.*

Booleans, integers, floats, and strings are the most important basic data types in Python. But often, you'll need to *structure* data items rather than just create them. In those cases, container types are the answer. But before we dive into container data structures, let's quickly learn about an important special data type: None.

The Keyword None

The keyword None is a Python constant and it means *the absence of a value.* Other programming languages such as Java use the value null instead. However, the term null often confuses beginners, who assume it's equal to the integer value 0. Instead, Python uses the keyword None, as shown as Listing 1-6, to indicate that it's different from any numerical value for zero, an empty list, or an empty string. An interesting fact is that the value None is the only value in the NoneType data type.

```
def f():
    x = 2


# The keyword 'is' will be introduced next
print(f() is None)
```

```
# True

print("" == None)
# False

print(0 == None)
# False
```

Listing 1-6: Using the keyword None

This code shows several examples of the None data value (and what it is not). If you don't define a return value for a function, the default return value is None.

Container Data Structures

Python ships with *container data types* that can handle complex operations efficiently while being easy to use.

Lists

The *list* is a container data type that stores a sequence of elements. Unlike strings, lists are *mutable*—you can modify them at runtime. I can best describe the list data type with a series of examples:

```
l = [1, 2, 2]
print(len(l))
# 3
```

This code snippet shows how to create a list by using square brackets and how to populate it with three integer elements. You can also see that lists can have repeated elements. The len() function returns the number of elements in a list.

Keyword: is

The keyword is simply checks whether both variables refer to the same object in memory. This can confuse Python newcomers. Listing 1-7 checks whether two integers and two lists refer to the same object in memory.

```
y = x = 3

print(x is y)
# True

print([3] is [3])
# False
```

Listing 1-7: Using the keyword is

If you create two lists—even if they contain the same elements—they still refer to two different list objects in memory. Modifying one list object does not affect the other list object. We say that lists are *mutable* because you can modify them after creation. Therefore, if you check whether one list refers to the same object in memory, the result is False. However, integer values are *immutable*, so there is no risk of one variable changing the object that will then accidentally change all other variables. The reason is that you cannot change the integer object 3—trying it will only create a new integer object and leave the old one unmodified.

Adding Elements

Python provides three common ways to add elements to an existing list: *append, insert,* or *list concatenation.*

```
# 1. Append
l = [1, 2, 2]
l.append(4)
print(l)
# [1, 2, 2, 4]

# 2. Insert
l = [1, 2, 4]
l.insert(2, 3)
print(l)
# [1, 2, 3, 4]

# 3. List Concatenation
print([1, 2, 2] + [4])
# [1, 2, 2, 4]
```

All three operations generate the same list [1, 2, 2, 4]. But the *append* operation is the fastest because it neither has to traverse the list to insert an element at the correct position (as with *insert*), nor create a new list out of two sublists (as with *list concatenation*). Roughly speaking, you use the insert operation only if you want to add an element at a specific position in the list that is not the last position. And you use the list concatenation operation to concatenate two lists of arbitrary length. Note that a fourth method, extend(), allows you to append multiple elements to the given list in an efficient manner.

Removing Elements

You can easily remove an element *x* from a list by using the list method remove(*x*):

```
l = [1, 2, 2, 4]
l.remove(1)
print(l)
# [2, 2, 4]
```

The method operates on the list object itself, rather than creating a new list with the changes made. In the previous code example, we create a list object named 1 and modify this exact object in memory by removing an element. This saves memory overhead by reducing redundant copies of the same list data.

Reversing Lists

You can reverse the order of list elements by using the method list.reverse():

```
l = [1, 2, 2, 4]
l.reverse()
print(l)
# [4, 2, 2, 1]
```

Reversing the list also modifies the original list object and does not merely create a new list object.

Sorting Lists

You can sort list elements by using the method list.sort():

```
l = [2, 1, 4, 2]
l.sort()
print(l)
# [1, 2, 2, 4]
```

Again, sorting the list modifies the original list object. The resulting list is sorted in an ascending manner. Lists containing string objects would be sorted in an ascending lexicographical manner (from 'a' to 'z'). In general, the sorting function assumes that two objects can be compared. Roughly speaking, if you can calculate a > b for objects a and b of any data type, Python can also sort the list [a, b].

Indexing List Elements

You can find out the index of a specified list element x by using the method list.index(x):

```
print([2, 2, 4].index(2))
# 0
```

```
print([2, 2, 4].index(2,1))
# 1
```

The method index(x) finds the first occurrence of the element x in the list and returns its index. Like other major programming languages, Python assigns index 0 to the first sequence and index $i-1$ to the i-th sequence.

Stacks

The *stack* data structure works intuitively as a first-in, first-out (FIFO) structure. Think of it as a stack of paperwork: you place every new paper on the top of a pile of old papers, and when you work through the stack, you keep removing the topmost document. The stack is still a fundamental data structure in computer science, used in operating system management, algorithms, syntax parsing, and backtracking.

Python lists can be used intuitively as stacks with the list operations append() to add to the stack and pop() to remove the most recently added item:

```
stack = [3]
stack.append(42) # [3, 42]
stack.pop() # 42 (stack: [3])
stack.pop() # 3 (stack: [])
```

Because of the efficiency of the list implementation, there is usually no need to import external stack libraries.

Sets

The *set* data structure is a basic collection data type in Python and many other programming languages. Popular languages for distributed computing (for example, MapReduce or Apache Spark) even focus almost exclusively on set operations as programming primitives. So what is a set exactly? A set is an unordered collection of unique elements. Let's break this definition into its main pieces.

Collection

A set is a collection of elements like a list or a tuple. The collection consists of either primitive elements (integers, floats, strings), or complex elements (objects, tuples). However, all data types in a set must be *hashable*, meaning that they have an associated hash value. A hash value of an object never changes and is used to compare the object to other objects. Let's look at an example in Listing 1-8, which creates a set from three strings after checking their hash values. You try to create a set of lists, but fail because lists are not hashable.

```
hero = "Harry"
guide = "Dumbledore"
enemy = "Lord V."
print(hash(hero))
# 6175908009919104006

print(hash(guide))
# -5197671124693729851

## Can we create a set of strings?
characters = {hero, guide, enemy}
print(characters)
# {'Lord V.', 'Dumbledore', 'Harry'}

## Can we create a set of lists?
team_1 = [hero, guide]
```

```
team_2 = [enemy]
teams = {team_1, team_2}
# TypeError: unhashable type: 'list'
```

Listing 1-8: The set data type allows for only hashable elements.

You can create a set of strings because strings are *hashable*. But you cannot create a set of lists, because lists are *unhashable*. The reason is that the hash value depends on the content of the item, and lists are *mutable*; if you change the list data type, the hash value must change too. Because mutable data types are not hashable, you cannot use them in sets.

Unordered

Unlike lists, elements in a set have no fixed order. Regardless of the order in which you put stuff into the set, you can never be sure in which order the set stores these elements. Here is an example:

```
characters = {hero, guide, enemy}
print(characters)
# {'Lord V.', 'Dumbledore', 'Harry'}
```

I put in the hero first, but my interpreter prints the enemy first (the Python interpreter is on the dark side, obviously). Note that your interpreter may print yet another order of the set elements.

Unique

All elements in the set must be unique. Formally, each of two values x, y in the set with $x!=y$ have different hash values $hash(x)!=hash(y)$. Because every two elements x and y in the set are different, you cannot create an army of Harry Potter clones to fight Lord V.:

```
clone_army = {hero, hero, hero, hero, hero, enemy}
print(clone_army)
# {'Lord V.', 'Harry'}
```

No matter how often you put the same value into the same set, the set stores only one instance of this value. The reason is that those heroes have the same hash value, and a set contains at most one element per hash value. An extension of the normal set data structure is the *multiset data structure*, which can store multiple instances of the same value. However, it is seldom used in practice. In contrast, you will use sets in almost any nontrivial code project—for example, to intersect a set of customers with a set of persons who visited a store, which will return a new set of customers who also visited the store.

Dictionaries

The *dictionary* is a useful data structure for storing (*key*, *value*) pairs:

```
calories = {'apple' : 52, 'banana' : 89, 'choco' : 546}
```

You can read and write elements by specifying the key within brackets:

```
print(calories['apple'] < calories['choco'])
# True

calories['cappu'] = 74

print(calories['banana'] < calories['cappu'])
# False
```

Use the keys() and values() functions to access all keys and values of the dictionary:

```
print('apple' in calories.keys())
# True

print(52 in calories.values())
# True
```

Access the (*key, value*) pairs of a dictionary with the items() method:

```
for k, v in calories.items():
    print(k) if v > 500 else None
# 'choco'
```

This way, it's easy to iterate over all keys and all values in a dictionary without accessing them individually.

Membership

Use the keyword in to check whether the set, list, or dictionary contains an element (see Listing 1-9).

```
❶ print(42 in [2, 39, 42])
  # True

❷ print("21" in {"2", "39", "42"})
  # False

  print("list" in {"list" : [1, 2, 3], "set" : {1,2,3}})
  # True
```

Listing 1-9: Using the keyword in

You use the keyword in to test membership of the integer value 42 ❶ in a list of integer values or to test membership of a string value "21" in a set of strings ❷. We say *x* is a *member* of *y* if element *x* appears in the collection *y*.

Checking set membership is faster than checking list membership: to check whether element *x* appears in list *y*, you need to traverse the whole list until you find *x* or have checked all elements. However, sets are implemented much like dictionaries: to check whether element *x* appears in set *y*, Python internally performs one operation $y[hash(x)]$ and checks whether the return value is not None.

List and Set Comprehension

List comprehension is a popular Python feature that helps you quickly create and modify lists. The simple formula is [*expression* + *context*]:

Expression   Tells Python what to do with each element in the list.

Context   Tells Python which list elements to select. The context consists of an arbitrary number of for and if statements.

For example, in the list comprehension statement [x for x in range(3)], the first part x is the (identity) expression, and the second part for x in range(3) is the context. The statement creates the list [0, 1, 2]. The range() function returns a range of subsequent integer values 0, 1, and 2—when used with one argument as in the example. Another code example for list comprehension is the following:

```
# (name, $-income)
customers = [("John", 240000),
             ("Alice", 120000),
             ("Ann", 1100000),
             ("Zach", 44000)]

# your high-value customers earning >$1M
whales = [x for x,y in customers if y>1000000]
print(whales)
# ['Ann']
```

Set comprehension is like list comprehension, but creates a set rather than a list.

Control Flow

Control flow functionality allows you to make decisions in your code. Algorithms are often compared to cooking recipes that consist of a sequential list of commands: fill the pot with water, add salt, add rice, drain the water, and serve the rice. As it is, without a *conditional execution*, the sequence of commands would take only a few seconds to execute, and the rice would not be ready for sure. For example, you would fill in water, salt, and rice and immediately get rid of the water without waiting for the water to be hot and the rice to be soft.

You need to respond in a different way to different circumstances: you need to put the rice in the pot only *if* the water is hot, and you need to remove the water from the pot only *if* the rice is soft. It's almost impossible to write programs in a way that anticipates what happens deterministically in the real world. Instead, you need to write programs that respond differently if different conditions are met.

if, else, and elif

The keywords if, else, and elif (see Listing 1-10) enable you to perform conditional execution of different code branches.

```
❶ x = int(input("your value: "))
❷ if x > 3:
      print("Big")
❸ elif x == 3:
      print("Medium")
❹ else:
      print("Small")
```

Listing 1-10: Using the keywords if, else, and elif

This first takes the user input, converts it into an integer, and stores it in the variable x ❶. It then tests whether the variable value is larger than ❷, equal to ❸, or smaller than ❹ the value 3. In other words, the code responds to real-world input that is *unpredictable* in a differentiated manner.

Loops

To allow for repeated execution of code snippets, Python uses two types of loops: for loops and while loops. Using these, you can easily write a program consisting only of two lines of code that execute forever. This repetition would be difficult otherwise (an alternative is *recursion.*)

In Listing 1-11, you can see both loop variants in action.

```
# For loop declaration
for i in [0, 1, 2]:
   print(i)

'''
0
1
2
'''


# While loop - same semantics
j = 0
while j < 3:
   print(j)
   j = j + 1

'''
0
1
2
'''
```

Listing 1-11: Using the keywords for and while

Both loop variants print the integers 0, 1, and 2 to the shell, but accomplish the task in two ways.

The for loop declares a loop variable i that iteratively takes on all values in the list [0, 1, 2]. It keeps running until it runs out of values.

The while loop executes the loop body as long as a particular condition is met—in our case, while j < 3.

There are two fundamental ways of terminating a loop: you can define a loop condition that eventually evaluates to False, or use the keyword break at the exact position in the loop body. Listing 1-12 shows an example of the latter.

```
while True:
    break # no infinite loop

print("hello world")
# hello world
```

Listing 1-12: Using the keyword break

You create a while loop with a loop condition that will always evaluate to True. So, at first sight, it seems to run forever. An infinite while loop is common practice when, for example, developing web servers that forever repeat the following procedure: wait for a new web request and serve the request. However, in some cases, you'll still want to terminate the loop prematurely. In the web server example, you would stop serving files for security reasons when your server detects that it is under attack. In these cases, you can use the keyword break to stop the loop and execute the code that follows immediately. In Listing 1-12, the code executes print("hello world") after the loop ends prematurely.

It is also possible to force the Python interpreter to skip certain areas in the loop without ending it prematurely. For example, you may want to skip malicious web requests instead of halting the server completely. You can achieve this by using the continue statement, which finishes the current loop iteration and brings the execution flow back to the loop condition (see Listing 1-13).

```
while True:
    continue
    print("43") # dead code
```

Listing 1-13: Using the keyword continue

This code executes forever without executing the print statement once. The reason is that the continue statement finishes the current loop iteration and takes it back to the start, so execution never reaches the print statement. Code that never executes is known as *dead code*. For this reason, the continue statement (as well as the break statement) is commonly used under a certain condition by using a conditional if-else environment.

Functions

Functions help you to reuse code snippets at your leisure: write them once but use them often. You define a function with the keyword def, a function name, and a set of arguments to customize the execution of the function body. Calling the function with two sets of arguments can drastically change the result of the function. For example, you can define the function square(x) that returns the square number of input argument *x*. Calling square(10) results in *10 × 10 = 100* while calling square(100) results in *100 × 100 = 10,000*.

The keyword return terminates the function and passes the flow of execution to the caller of the function. You can also provide an optional value after the return keyword to specify the function result (see Listing 1-14).

```
def appreciate(x, percentage):
    return x + x * percentage / 100


print(appreciate(10000, 5))
# 10500.0
```

Listing 1-14: Using the keyword return

You create a function appreciate() that calculates how much a given investment appreciates at a given percentage of return. In the code, you calculate how much an investment of $10,000 appreciates in one year when assuming an interest rate of 5 percent. The result is $10,500. You use the keyword return to specify that the result of the function should be the sum of the original investment and the nominal interest of this investment. The return value of the function appreciate() is of type float.

Lambdas

You use the keyword lambda to define lambda functions in Python. *Lambda functions* are anonymous functions that are not defined in the namespace. Roughly speaking, they are functions without names, intended for single use. The syntax is as follows:

```
lambda <arguments> : <return expression>
```

A lambda function can have one or multiple arguments, separated by commas. After the colon (:), you define the return expression that may (or may not) use the defined argument. The return expression can be any expression or even another function.

Lambda functions play a major role in Python. You'll see them a lot in practical code projects: for example, to make code shorter and more concise, or to create arguments of various Python functions (such as map() or reduce()). Consider the code in Listing 1-15.

```
print((lambda x: x + 3)(3))
# 6
```

Listing 1-15: Using the keyword lambda

First, you create a lambda function that takes a value x and returns the result of the expression x + 3. The result is a function object that can be called like any other function. Because of its semantics, you denote this function as an *incrementor function*. When calling this incrementor function with the argument x=3—the suffix (3) within the print statement in Listing 1-15—the result is the integer value 6. This book uses lambda functions heavily, so make sure you understand them properly (though you will also have opportunities to improve your intuitive understanding of lambda functions).

Summary

This chapter gave you a concise Python crash course to refresh your basic Python education. You studied the most important Python data structures and how to use them in code examples. You learned how to control the program execution flow by using if-elif-else statements, as well as while and for loops. You revisited the basic data types in Python—Boolean, integer, float, and string—and saw which built-in operations and functions are commonly used. Most code snippets in practice and nontrivial algorithms are built around more-powerful container types such as lists, stacks, sets, and dictionaries. By studying the given examples, you learned how to add, remove, insert, and reorder elements. You also learned about membership operators and list comprehension: an efficient and powerful built-in method to create lists programmatically in Python. Finally, you learned about functions and how to define them (including the anonymous lambda function). Now, you are ready for the first 10 basic Python one-liners.

2

PYTHON TRICKS

For our purposes, a *trick* is a way of accomplishing a task in a surprisingly fast or easy manner. In this book, you'll learn a wide variety of tricks and techniques to make your code more concise, while boosting your speed of implementation. While all technical chapters in this book show you Python tricks, this chapter addresses the low-hanging fruit: tricks you can adopt quickly and effortlessly, but with great effect on your coding productivity.

This chapter also serves as a stepping-stone for the more advanced chapters that follow. You need to understand the skills introduced in these one-liners to understand those that follow. Notably, we'll cover a range of basic Python functionality to help you write effective code, including list comprehension, file access, the map() function, the lambda function, the reduce() function, slicing, slice assignments, generator functions, and the zip() function.

If you're already an advanced programmer, you could skim over this chapter and decide which individual parts you want to study in more depth—and which ones you already understand well.

Using List Comprehension to Find Top Earners

In this section, you'll learn a beautiful, powerful, and highly efficient Python feature to create lists: list comprehension. You'll use list comprehension in many of the one-liners to come.

The Basics

Say you work in the human resources department of a large company and need to find all staff members who earn at least $100,000 per year. Your desired output is a list of tuples, each consisting of two values: the employee name and the employee's yearly salary. Here's the code you develop:

```
employees = {'Alice' : 100000,
             'Bob' : 99817,
             'Carol' : 122908,
             'Frank' : 88123,
             'Eve' : 93121}


top_earners = []
for key, val in employees.items():
    if val >= 100000:
        top_earners.append((key,val))

print(top_earners)
# [('Alice', 100000), ('Carol', 122908)]
```

While the code is correct, there's an easier and much more concise—and therefore more readable—way of accomplishing the same result. All things being equal, the solution with *fewer lines* allows the reader to grasp the meaning of code faster.

Python offers a powerful way of creating new lists: *list comprehension*. The simple formula is as follows:

```
[ expression + context ]
```

The enclosing brackets indicate that the result is a new list. The *context* defines which list elements to select. The *expression* defines how to modify each list element before adding the result to the list. Here's an example:

```
[x * 2 for x in range(3)]
```

The bold part of the equation, `for x in range(3)`, is the context and the remaining part `x * 2`, is the expression. Roughly speaking, the expression doubles the values 0, 1, 2 generated by the context. Thus, the list comprehension results in the following list:

```
[0, 2, 4]
```

Both the expression and the context can be arbitrarily complicated. The expression may be a function of any variable defined in the context and may perform any computation—it can even call outside functions. The goal of the expression is to modify each list element before adding it to the new list.

The context can consist of one or many variables defined using one or many nested for loops. You can also restrict the context by using if statements. In this case, a new value will be added to the list only if the user-defined condition holds.

List comprehension is best explained by example. Study the following examples carefully and you'll get a good sense of list comprehension:

```
print([❶x ❷for x in range(5)])
# [0, 1, 2, 3, 4]
```

Expression ❶: Identity function (does not change the context variable x).
Context ❷: Context variable x takes all values returned by the range function: 0, 1, 2, 3, 4.

```
print([❶(x, y) ❷for x in range(3) for y in range(3)])
# [(0, 0), (0, 1), (0, 2), (1, 0), (1, 1), (1, 2), (2, 0), (2, 1), (2, 2)]
```

Expression ❶: Create a new tuple from the context variables x and y.
Context ❷: The context variable x iterates over all values returned by the range function (0, 1, 2), while context variable y iterates over all values returned by the range function (0, 1, 2). The two for loops are nested, so the context variable y repeats its iteration procedure for every single value of the context variable x. Thus, there are 3 × 3 = 9 combinations of context variables.

```
print([❶x ** 2 ❷for x in range(10) if x % 2 > 0])
# [1, 9, 25, 49, 81]
```

Expression ❶: Square function on the context variable x.
Context ❷: Context variable x iterates over all values returned by the range function—0, 1, 2, 3, 4, 5, 6, 7, 8, 9—but only if they are odd values; that is, x % 2 > 0.

```
print([❶x.lower() ❷for x in ['I', 'AM', 'NOT', 'SHOUTING']])
# ['i', 'am', 'not', 'shouting']
```

Expression ❶: String lowercase function on context variable x.

Context ❷: Context variable x iterates over all string values in the list: `'I'`, `'AM'`, `'NOT'`, `'SHOUTING'`.

Now, you should be able to understand the following code snippet.

The Code

Let's consider the same employee salary problem introduced earlier: given a dictionary with string keys and integer values, create a new list of (key, value) tuples so that the value associated with the key is larger than or equal to 100,000. Listing 2-1 shows the code.

```
## Data
employees = {'Alice' : 100000,
             'Bob' : 99817,
             'Carol' : 122908,
             'Frank' : 88123,
             'Eve' : 93121}


## One-Liner
top_earners = [(k, v) for k, v in employees.items() if v >= 100000]


## Result
print(top_earners)
```

Listing 2-1: One-liner solution for list comprehension

What's the output of this code snippet?

How It Works

Let's examine the one-liner:

```
top_earners = [ ❶(k, v) ❷for k, v in employees.items() if v >= 100000]
```

Expression ❶: Creates a simple (key, value) tuple for context variables k and v.

Context ❷: The dictionary method `dict.items()` ensures that context variable k iterates over all dictionary keys and that context variable v iterates over the associated values for context variable k—but only if the value of context variable v is larger than or equal to 100,000 as ensured by the if condition.

The result of the one-liner is as follows:

```
print(top_earners)
# [('Alice', 100000), ('Carol', 122908)]
```

This simple one-liner program introduces the important concept of *list comprehension*. We use list comprehension in multiple instances in this book, so make sure that you understand the examples in this section before moving on.

Using List Comprehension to Find Words with High Information Value

In this one-liner, you'll dive even deeper into the powerful feature of list comprehension.

The Basics

Search engines rank textual information according to its relevance to a user query. To accomplish this, search engines analyze the content of the text to be searched. All text consists of words. Some words provide a lot of information about the content of the text—and others don't. Examples for the former are words like *white, whale, Captain, Ahab* (Do you know the text?). Examples for the latter are words like *is, to, as, the, a,* or *how,* because most texts contain those words. Filtering out words that don't contribute a lot of meaning is common practice when implementing search engines. A simple heuristic is to filter out all words with three characters or less.

The Code

Our goal is to solve the following problem: given a multiline string, create a list of lists—each consisting of all the words in a line that have more than three characters. Listing 2-2 provides the data and the solution.

```
## Data
text = '''
Call me Ishmael. Some years ago - never mind how long precisely - having
little or no money in my purse, and nothing particular to interest me
on shore, I thought I would sail about a little and see the watery part
of the world. It is a way I have of driving off the spleen, and regulating
the circulation. - Moby Dick'''


## One-Liner
w = [[x for x in line.split() if len(x)>3] for line in text.split('\n')]


## Result
print(w)
```

Listing 2-2: One-liner solution to find words with high information value

What's the output of this code?

How It Works

The one-liner creates a list of lists by using two nested list comprehension expressions:

- The inner list comprehension expression [x for x in line.split() if len(x)>3] uses the string split() function to divide a given line into a sequence of words. We iterate over all words x and add them to the list if they have more than three characters.
- The outer list comprehension expression creates the string line used in the previous statement. Again, it uses the split() function to divide the text on the newline characters '\n'.

Of course, you need to get used to thinking in terms of list comprehensions, so the meaning may not come naturally to you. But after reading this book, list comprehensions will be your bread and butter—and you'll quickly read and write Pythonic code like this.

Reading a File

In this section, you'll read a file and store the result as a list of strings (one string per line). You'll also remove any leading and trailing whitespaces from the lines.

The Basics

In Python, reading a file is straightforward but usually takes a few lines of code (and one or two Google searches) to accomplish. Here's one standard way of reading a file in Python:

```
filename = "readFileDefault.py" # this code

f = open(filename)
lines = []
for line in f:
    lines.append(line.strip())

print(lines)
"""
['filename = "readFileDefault.py" # this code',
'',
'f = open(filename)',
'lines = []',
'for line in f:',
'lines.append(line.strip())',
'',
'print(lines)']
"""
```

The code assumes that you've stored this code snippet in a file named *readFileDefault.py* in a folder. The code then opens this file, creates an empty list, lines, and fills the list with strings by using the append() operation in the for loop body to iterate over all the lines in the file. You also use the string method strip() to remove any leading or trailing whitespace (otherwise, the newline character '\n' would appear in the strings).

To access files on your computer, you need to know how to open and close files. You can access a file's data only after you've opened it. After closing the file, you can be sure that the data was written into the file. Python may create a buffer and wait for a while before it writes the whole buffer into the file (Figure 2-1). The reason for this is simple: file access is slow. For efficiency reasons, Python avoids writing every single bit independently. Instead, it waits until the buffer has filled with enough bytes and then flushes the whole buffer at once into the file.

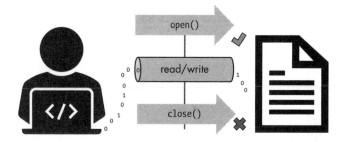

Figure 2-1: Opening and closing a file in Python

That's why it's good practice to close the file after reading it with the command f.close(), to ensure all the data is properly written into the file instead of residing in temporary memory. However, in a few exceptions, Python closes the file automatically: one of these exceptions occurs when the reference count drops to zero, as you'll see in the following code.

The Code

Our goal is to open a file, read all lines, strip the leading and trailing whitespace characters, and store the result in a list. Listing 2-3 provides the one-liner.

```
print([line.strip() for line in open("readFile.py")])
```

Listing 2-3: One-liner solution to read a file line by line.

Go ahead and guess the output of this code snippet before reading on.

How It Works

You use the print() statement to print the resulting list to the shell. You create the list by using list comprehension (see "Using List Comprehension to Find Top Earners" on page 18). In the *expression* part of the list comprehension, you use the strip() method of string objects.

The *context* part of the list comprehension iterates over all lines in the file.

The output of the one-liner is simply the one-liner itself (because it reads its Python source code file with the name *readFile.py*), wrapped into a string and filled into a list:

```
print([line.strip() for line in open("readFile.py")])
# ['print([line.strip() for line in open("readFile.py")])']
```

This section demonstrates that by making code shorter and more concise, you make it more readable without compromising efficiency.

Using Lambda and Map Functions

This section introduces two important Python features: the `lambda` and `map()` functions. Both functions are valuable tools in your Python toolbox. You'll use these functions to search a list of strings for occurrences of another string.

The Basics

In Chapter 1, you learned how to define a new function with the expression `def x`, followed by the content of the function. However, this is not the only way of defining a function in Python. You can also use *lambda functions* to define a simple function *with a return value* (the return value can be any object, including tuples, lists, and sets). In other words, every lambda function returns an object value to its calling environment. Note that this poses a practical restriction to lambda functions, because unlike standard functions, they are not designed to execute code *without* returning an object value to the calling environment.

NOTE *We already covered lambda functions in Chapter 1, but because it's such an important concept used throughout this book, we'll take a deeper look in this section.*

Lambda functions allow you to define a new function in a single line by using the keyword `lambda`. This is useful when you want to quickly create a function that you'll use only once and can be garbage-collected immediately afterward. Let's first study the exact syntax of lambda functions:

```
lambda arguments : return expression
```

You start the function definition with the keyword `lambda`, followed by a sequence of function arguments. When calling the function, the caller must provide these arguments. You then include a colon (:) and the *return expression*, which calculates the return value based on the arguments of the lambda function. The return expression calculates the function output and can be any Python expression. Consider the following function definition as an example:

```
lambda x, y: x + y
```

The lambda function has two arguments, x and y. The return value is simply the sum of both arguments, x + y.

You typically use a lambda function when you call the function only once and can easily define it in a single line of code. One common example is using lambda with the map() function that takes as input arguments a function object f and a sequence s. The map() function then applies the function f on each element in the sequence s. Of course, you *could* define a full-fledged named function to define the function argument f. But this is often inconvenient and reduces readability—especially if the function is short and you need it only once—so it's usually best to use a lambda function here.

Before presenting the one-liner, I'll quickly introduce another small Python trick that makes your life easier: checking whether string x contains substring y by using the expression y in x. This statement returns True if there exists at least one occurrence of the string y in the string x. For example, the expression '42' in 'The answer is 42' evaluates to True, while the expression '21' in 'The answer is 42' evaluates to False.

Now let's look at our one-liner.

The Code

When given a list of strings, our next one-liner (Listing 2-4) creates a new list of tuples, each consisting of a Boolean value and the original string. The Boolean value indicates whether the string 'anonymous' appears in the original string! We call the resulting list mark because the Boolean values *mark* the string elements in the list that contain the string 'anonymous'.

```
## Data
txt = ['lambda functions are anonymous functions.',
       'anonymous functions dont have a name.',
       'functions are objects in Python.']


## One-Liner
mark = map(lambda s: (True, s) if 'anonymous' in s else (False, s), txt)


## Result
print(list(mark))
```

Listing 2-4: One-liner solution to mark strings that contain the string 'anonymous'

What's the output of this code?

How It Works

The map() function adds a Boolean value to each string element in the original txt list. This Boolean value is True if the string element contains the word *anonymous*. The first argument is the anonymous lambda function, and the second is a list of strings you want to check for the desired string.

You use the lambda return expression (True, s) if 'anonymous' in s else (False, s) to search for the 'anonymous' string. The value s is the input argument of the lambda function, which, in this example, is a string. If the string query 'anonymous' exists in the string, the expression returns the tuple (True, s). Otherwise, it returns the tuple (False, s).

The result of the one-liner is the following:

```
## Result
print(list(mark))
# [(True, 'lambda functions are anonymous functions.'),
# (True, 'anonymous functions dont have a name.'),
# (False, 'functions are objects in Python.')]
```

The Boolean values indicate that only the first two strings in the list contain the substring 'anonymous'.

You'll find lambdas incredibly useful in the upcoming one-liners. You're also making consistent progress toward your goal: understanding every single line of Python code you'll encounter in practice.

EXERCISE 2-1

Use list comprehension rather than the map() function to accomplish the same output. (You can find the solution at the end of this chapter.)

Using Slicing to Extract Matching Substring Environments

This section teaches you the important basic concept of *slicing*—the process of carving out a subsequence from an original full sequence—to process simple text queries. We'll search some text for a specific string, and then extract that string along with a handful of characters around it to give us context.

The Basics

Slicing is integral to a vast number of Python concepts and skills, both advanced and basic, such as when using any of Python's built-in data structures like lists, tuples, and strings. Slicing is also the basis of many advanced Python libraries such as NumPy, Pandas, TensorFlow, and scikit-learn. Studying slicing thoroughly will have a positive ripple effect throughout your career as a Python coder.

Slicing carves out subsequences of a sequence, such as a part of a string. The syntax is straightforward. Say you have a variable x that refers to a string, list, or tuple. You can carve out a subsequence by using the following notation:

```
x[start:stop:step].
```

The resulting subsequence starts at index start (included) and ends at index stop (excluded). You can include an optional third step argument that determines which elements are carved out, so you could choose to include just every step-th element. For example, the slicing operation x[1:4:1] used on variable x = 'hello world' results in the string 'ell'. Slicing operation x[1:4:2] on the same variable results in string 'el' because only every other element is taken into the resulting slice. Recall from Chapter 1 that the first element of any sequence type, such as strings and lists, has index 0 in Python.

If you don't include the step argument, Python assumes the default step size of one. For example, the slice call x[1:4] would result in the string 'ell'.

If you don't include the beginning or ending arguments, Python assumes you want to start at the start, or end at the end. For example, the slice call x[:4] would result in the string 'hell', and the slice call x[4:] would result in the string 'o world'.

Study the following examples to improve your intuitive understanding even further.

```
s = 'Eat more fruits!'

print(s[0:3])
# Eat
```

❶
```
print(s[3:0])
# (empty string '')
```

```
print(s[:5])
# Eat m
```

```
print(s[5:])
# ore fruits!
```

❷
```
print(s[:100])
# Eat more fruits!
```

```
print(s[4:8:2])
# mr
```

❸
```
print(s[::3])
# E rfi!
```

❹
```
print(s[::-1])
# !stiurf erom taE
```

```
print(s[6:1:-1])
# rom t
```

These variants of the basic [start:stop:step] pattern of Python slicing highlight the technique's many interesting properties:

- If start >= stop with a positive step size, the slice is empty ❶.
- If the stop argument is larger than the sequence length, Python will slice all the way to and including the rightmost element ❷.
- If the step size is positive, the default start is the leftmost element, and the default stop is the rightmost element (included) ❸.
- If the step size is negative (step < 0), the slice traverses the sequence in reverse order. With empty start and stop arguments, you slice from the rightmost element (included) to the leftmost element (included) ❹. Note that if the stop argument is given, the respective position is excluded from the slice.

Next, you'll use slicing along with the string.find(value) method to find the index of string argument value in a given string.

The Code

Our goal is to find a particular text query within a multiline string. You want to find the query in the text and return its immediate environment, up to 18 positions around the found query. Extracting the environment as well as the query is useful for seeing the textual context of the found string—just as Google presents text snippets around a searched keyword. In Listing 2-5, you're looking for the string 'SQL' in an Amazon letter to shareholders—with the immediate environment of up to 18 positions around the string 'SQL'.

```
## Data
letters_amazon = '''
We spent several years building our own database engine,
Amazon Aurora, a fully-managed MySQL and PostgreSQL-compatible
service with the same or better durability and availability as
the commercial engines, but at one-tenth of the cost. We were
not surprised when this worked.
'''

## One-Liner
find = lambda x, q: x[x.find(q)-18:x.find(q)+18] if q in x else -1

## Result
print(find(letters_amazon, 'SQL'))
```

Listing 2-5: One-liner solution to find strings in a text and their direct environment

Take a guess at the output of this code.

How It Works

You define a lambda function with two arguments: a string value x, and a query q to search for in the text. You assign the lambda function to the name find. The function find(x, q) finds the string query q in the string text x.

If the query q does not appear in the string x, you directly return the result -1. Otherwise, you use slicing on the text string to carve out the first occurrence of the query, plus 18 characters to the left of the query and 18 characters to the right, to capture the query's environment. You find that the index of the first occurrence of q in x is using the string function x.find(q). You call the function twice: to help determine the start index and the stop index of the slice, but both function calls return the same value because both the query q and the string x do not change. Although this code works perfectly fine, the redundant function call causes unnecessary computations—a disadvantage that could easily be fixed by adding a helper variable to temporarily store the result of the first function call. You could then reuse the result from the first function call by accessing the value in the helper variable.

This discussion highlights an important trade-off: by restricting yourself to one line of code, you cannot define and reuse a helper variable to store the index of the first occurrence of the query. Instead, you must execute the same function find to compute the start index (and decrement the result by 18 index positions) and to compute the end index (and increment the result by 18 index positions). In Chapter 5, you'll learn a more efficient way of searching patterns in strings (using regular expressions) that resolves this issue.

When searching for the query 'SQL' in Amazon's letter to shareholders, you find an occurrence of the query in the text:

```
## Result
print(find(letters_amazon, 'SQL'))
# a fully-managed MySQL and PostgreSQL
```

As a result, you get the string and a few words around it to provide context for the find. Slicing is a crucial element of your basic Python education. Let's deepen your understanding even more with another slicing one-liner.

Combining List Comprehension and Slicing

This section combines list comprehension and slicing to sample a two-dimensional data set. We aim to create a smaller but representative sample of data from a prohibitively large sample.

The Basics

Say you work as a financial analyst for a large bank and are training a new machine learning model for stock-price forecasting. You have a training data set of real-world stock prices. However, the data set is huge, and the model training seems to take forever on your computer. For example, it's common in machine learning to test the prediction accuracy of your model for different sets of model parameters. In our application, say, you must wait for hours until the training program terminates (training highly complex models on large-scale data sets does in fact take hours). To speed things up, you reduce the data set by half by excluding every other stock-price data point. You don't expect this modification to decrease the model's accuracy significantly.

In this section, you'll use two Python features you learned about previously in this chapter: list comprehension and slicing. List comprehension allows you to iterate over each list element and modify it subsequently. Slicing allows you to select every other element from a given list quickly—and it lends itself naturally to simple filtering operations. Let's have a detailed look at how these two features can be used in combination.

The Code

Our goal is to create a new training data sample from our data—a list of lists, each consisting of six floats—by including only every other float value from the original data set. Take a look at Listing 2-6.

```
## Data (daily stock prices ($))
price = [[9.9, 9.8, 9.8, 9.4, 9.5, 9.7],
         [9.5, 9.4, 9.4, 9.3, 9.2, 9.1],
         [8.4, 7.9, 7.9, 8.1, 8.0, 8.0],
         [7.1, 5.9, 4.8, 4.8, 4.7, 3.9]]


## One-Liner
sample = [line[::2] for line in price]


## Result
print(sample)
```

Listing 2-6: One-liner solution to sample data

As usual, see if you can guess the output.

How It Works

Our solution is a two-step approach. First, you use list comprehension to iterate over all lines of the original list, price. Second, you create a new list of floats by slicing each line; you use line[start:stop:step] with default start and stop parameters and step size 2. The new list of floats consists of only three (instead of six) floats, resulting in the following array:

```
## Result
print(sample)
# [[9.9, 9.8, 9.5], [9.5, 9.4, 9.2], [8.4, 7.9, 8.0], [7.1, 4.8, 4.7]]
```

This one-liner using built-in Python functionality is not complicated. However, you'll learn about an even shorter version that uses the NumPy library for data science computations in Chapter 3.

Using Slice Assignment to Correct Corrupted Lists

This section shows you a powerful slicing feature in Python: slice assignments. *Slice assignments* use slicing notation *on the left-hand side* of an assignment operation to modify a subsequence of the original sequence.

The Basics

Imagine you work at a small internet startup that keeps track of its users' web browsers (Google Chrome, Firefox, Safari). You store the data in a database. To analyze the data, you load the gathered browser data into a large list of strings, but because of a bug in your tracking algorithm, every second string is corrupted and needs to be replaced by the correct string.

Assume that your web server always redirects the first web request of a user to another URL (this is a common practice in web development known under the HTML code 301: *moved permanently*). You conclude that the first browser value will be equal to the second one in most cases because the browser of a user stays the same while waiting for the redirection to occur. This means that you can easily reproduce the original data. Essentially, you want to duplicate every other string in the list: the list ['Firefox', 'corrupted', 'Chrome', 'corrupted'] becomes ['Firefox', 'Firefox', 'Chrome', 'Chrome'].

How can you achieve this in a fast, readable, and efficient way (preferably in a single line of code)? Your first idea is to create a new list, iterate over the corrupted list, and add every noncorrupted browser twice to the new list. But you reject the idea because you'd then have to maintain two lists in your code—and each may have millions of entries. Also, this solution would require a few lines of code, which would hurt conciseness and readability of your source code.

Luckily, you've read about a beautiful Python feature: slice assignments. You'll use slice assignments to select and replace a *sequence of elements* between indices i and j by using the slicing notation lst[i:j] = [0 0 ...0]. Because you are using slicing lst[i:j] on the *left-hand side* of the assignment operation (rather than on the right-hand side as done previously), the feature is denoted as slice *assignments*.

The idea of slice assignments is simple: replace all selected elements in the original sequence on the left with the elements on the right.

The Code

Our goal is to replace every other string with the string immediately in front of it; see Listing 2-7.

```
## Data
visitors = ['Firefox', 'corrupted', 'Chrome', 'corrupted',
            'Safari', 'corrupted', 'Safari', 'corrupted',
            'Chrome', 'corrupted', 'Firefox', 'corrupted']


## One-Liner
visitors[1::2] = visitors[::2]


## Result
print(visitors)
```

Listing 2-7: One-liner solution to replace all corrupted strings

What's the fixed sequence of browsers in this code?

How It Works

The one-liner solution replaces the 'corrupted' strings with the browser strings that precede them in the list. You use the slice assignment notation to access every corrupted element in the visitors list. I've highlighted the selected elements in the following code snippet:

```
visitors = ['Firefox', 'corrupted', 'Chrome', 'corrupted',
            'Safari', 'corrupted', 'Safari', 'corrupted',
            'Chrome', 'corrupted', 'Firefox', 'corrupted']
```

The code replaces these selected elements with the slice on the right of the assignment operation. These elements are highlighted in the following code snippet:

```
visitors = ['Firefox', 'corrupted', 'Chrome', 'corrupted',
            'Safari', 'corrupted', 'Safari', 'corrupted',
            'Chrome', 'corrupted', 'Firefox', 'corrupted']
```

The former elements are replaced by the latter. Therefore, the resulting visitors list is the following (highlighting the replaced elements):

```
## Result
print(visitors)
'''
['Firefox', 'Firefox', 'Chrome', 'Chrome',
'Safari', 'Safari', 'Safari', 'Safari',
'Chrome', 'Chrome', 'Firefox', 'Firefox']
'''
```

The result is the original list with each 'corrupted' string replaced by its preceding browser string. This way, you clean the corrupted data set.

Using slice assignments for this problem is the quickest and most effective way of accomplishing your small task. Note that the cleaned data has nonbiased browser usage statistics: a browser with 70 percent market share in the corrupted data will maintain its 70 percent market share in the cleaned data. The cleaned data can then be used for further analysis—for example, to find out whether Safari users are better customers (after all, they tend to spend more money on hardware). You've learned a simple and concise way of modifying a list programmatically and in place.

Analyzing Cardiac Health Data with List Concatenation

In this section, you'll learn how to use list concatenation to repeatedly copy smaller lists and merge them into a larger list to generate cyclic data.

The Basics

This time, you're working on a small code project for a hospital. Your goal is to monitor and visualize the health statistics of patients by tracking their cardiac cycles. By plotting expected cardiac cycle data, you'll enable patients and doctors to monitor any deviation from that cycle. For example, given a series of measurements stored in the list [62, 60, 62, 64, 68, 77, 80, 76, 71, 66, 61, 60, 62] for a single cardiac cycle, you want to achieve the visualization in Figure 2-2.

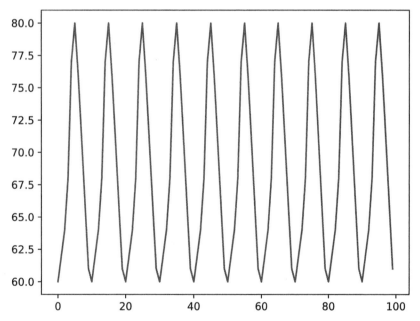

Figure 2-2: Visualizing expected cardiac cycles by copying selected values from the measured data

The problem is that the first and the last two data values in the list are redundant: [62, 60, 62, 64, 68, 77, 80, 76, 71, 66, 61, 60, 62]. This may have been useful when plotting only a single cardiac cycle to indicate that one full cycle has been visualized. However, we must get rid of this redundant data to ensure that our expected cardiac cycles do not look like the ones in Figure 2-3 when copying the same cardiac cycle.

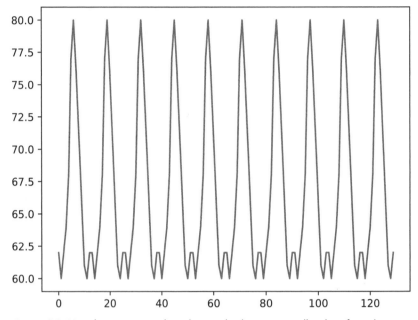

Figure 2-3: Visualizing expected cardiac cycles by copying all values from the measured data (no filtering of redundant data)

Clearly, you need to *clean* the original list by removing the redundant first and the last two data values: [62, 60, 62, 64, 68, 77, 80, 76, 71, 66, 61, 60, 62] becomes [60, 62, 64, 68, 77, 80, 76, 71, 66, 61].

You'll combine slicing with the new Python feature *list concatenation*, which creates a new list by *concatenating* (that is, *joining*) existing lists. For example, the operation [1, 2, 3] + [4, 5] generates the new list [1, 2, 3, 4, 5], but doesn't replace the original lists. You can use this with the * operator to concatenate the *same list* again and again to create large lists: for example, the operation [1, 2, 3] * 3 generates the new list [1, 2, 3, 1, 2, 3, 1, 2, 3].

In addition, you'll use the matplotlib.pyplot module to plot the cardiac data you generate. The matplotlib function plot(data) expects an iterable argument data—an *iterable* is simply an object over which you can iterate, such as a list—and uses it as y values for subsequent data points in a two-dimensional plot. Let's dive into the example.

The Code

Given a list of integers that reflect the measured cardiac cycle, you first want to clean the data by removing the first and last two values from the list. Second, you create a new list with expected future heart rates by copying the cardiac cycle to future time instances. Listing 2-8 shows the code.

```
## Dependencies
import matplotlib.pyplot as plt


## Data
cardiac_cycle = [62, 60, 62, 64, 68, 77, 80, 76, 71, 66, 61, 60, 62]


## One-Liner
expected_cycles = cardiac_cycle[1:-2] * 10


## Result
plt.plot(expected_cycles)
plt.show()
```

Listing 2-8: One-liner solution to predict heart rates at different times

Next, you'll learn about the result of this code snippet.

How It Works

This one-liner consists of two steps. First, you use slicing to clean the data by using the negative stop argument -2 to slice all the way to the right but skip the last two redundant values. Second, you concatenate the resulting data values 10 times by using the replication operator *. The result is a list of $10 \times 10 = 100$ integers made up of the concatenated cardiac cycle data. When you plot the result, you get the desired output shown previously in Figure 2-2.

Using Generator Expressions to Find Companies That Pay Below Minimum Wage

This section combines some of the Python basics you've already learned and introduces the useful function any().

The Basics

You work in law enforcement for the US Department of Labor, finding companies that pay below minimum wage so you can initiate further investigations. Like hungry dogs on the back of a meat truck, your Fair Labor Standards Act (FLSA) officers are already waiting for the list of companies that violated the minimum wage law. Can you give it to them?

Here's your weapon: Python's any() function, which takes an iterable, such as a list, and returns True if at least one element of the iterable evaluates to True. For example, the expression any([True, False, False, False]) evaluates to True, while the expression any([2<1, 3+2>5+5, 3-2<0, 0]) evaluates to False.

NOTE *Python's creator, Guido van Rossum, was a huge fan of the built-in function any() and even proposed to include it as a built-in function in Python 3. See his 2005 blog post, "The Fate of reduce() in Python 3000" at* https://www.artima.com /weblogs/viewpost.jsp?thread=98196 *for more details.*

An interesting Python extension is a generalization of list comprehension: generator expressions. *Generator expressions* work exactly like list comprehensions—but without creating an actual list in memory. The numbers are created on the fly, without storing them explicitly in a list. For example, instead of using list comprehension to calculate the squares of the first 20 numbers, sum([x*x for x in range(20)]), you can use a generator expression: sum(x*x for x in range(20)).

The Code

Our data is a dictionary of dictionaries storing the hourly wages of company employees. You want to extract a list of the companies paying below your state's minimum wage (< $9) for at least one employee; see Listing 2-9.

```
## Data
companies = {
    'CoolCompany' : {'Alice' : 33, 'Bob' : 28, 'Frank' : 29},
    'CheapCompany' : {'Ann' : 4, 'Lee' : 9, 'Chrisi' : 7},
    'SosoCompany' : {'Esther' : 38, 'Cole' : 8, 'Paris' : 18}}


## One-Liner
illegal = [x for x in companies if any(y<9 for y in companies[x].values())]


## Result
print(illegal)
```

Listing 2-9: One-liner solution to find companies that pay below minimum wage

Which companies must be further investigated?

How It Works

You use two generator expressions in this one-liner.

The first generator expression, y<9 for y in companies[x].values(), generates the input to the function any(). It checks each of the companies' employees to see whether they are being paid below minimum wage, y<9. The result is an iterable of Booleans. You use the dictionary function values() to return the collection of values stored in the dictionary. For example, the expression companies['CoolCompany'].values() returns the collection of hourly wages dict_values([33, 28, 29]). If at least one of them is below minimum wage, the function any() would return True, and the company name x would be stored as a string in the resulting list illegal, as described next.

The second generator expression is the list comprehension [x for x in companies if any(...)] and it creates a list of company names for which the previous call of the function any() returns True. Those are the companies that pay below minimum wage. Note that the expression for x in companies visits all dictionary keys—the company names 'CoolCompany', 'CheapCompany', and 'SosoCompany'.

The result is therefore as follows:

```
## Result
print(illegal)
# ['CheapCompany', 'SosoCompany']
```

Two out of three companies must be investigated further because they pay too little money to at least one employee. Your officers can start to talk to Ann, Chrisi, and Cole!

Formatting Databases with the zip() Function

In this section, you'll learn how to apply database column names to a list of rows by using the zip() function.

The Basics

The zip() function takes iterables iter_1, iter_2, ..., iter_n and aggregates them into a single iterable by aligning the corresponding i-th values into a single tuple. The result is an *iterable* of tuples. For example, consider these two lists:

```
[1,2,3]
[4,5,6]
```

If you zip them together—after a simple data type conversion, as you'll see in a moment—you'll get a new list:

```
[(1,4), (2,5), (3,6)]
```

Unzipping them back into the original tuples requires two steps. First, you remove the outer square bracket of the result to get the following three tuples:

```
(1,4)
(2,5)
(3,6)
```

Then when you zip those together, you get the new list:

```
[(1,2,3), (4,5,6)]
```

So, you have your two original lists again! The following code snippet shows this process in full:

```
lst_1 = [1, 2, 3]
lst_2 = [4, 5, 6]

# Zip two lists together
zipped = list(zip(lst_1, lst_2))
print(zipped)
# [(1, 4), (2, 5), (3, 6)]

# Unzip to lists again
lst_1_new, lst_2_new = zip(❶*zipped)
print(list(lst_1_new))
print(list(lst_2_new))
```

You use the asterisk operator * to unpack ❶ all elements of the list. This operator removes the outer bracket of the list zipped so that the input to the zip() function consists of three iterables (the tuples (1, 4), (2, 5), (3, 6)). If you zip those iterables together, you package the first three tuple values 1, 2, and 3 into a new tuple, and the second three tuple values 4, 5, and 6 into another new tuple. Together, you get the resulting iterables (1, 2, 3) and (4, 5, 6), which is the original (unzipped) data.

Now, imagine you work in the IT branch of the controlling department of your company. You maintain the database of all employees with the column names: 'name', 'salary', and 'job'. However, your data is out of shape—it's a collection of rows in the form ('Bob', 99000, 'mid-level manager'). You want to associate your column names to each data entry to bring it into the readable form {'name': 'Bob', 'salary': 99000, 'job': 'mid-level manager'}. How can you achieve that?

The Code

Your data consists of the column names and the employee data organized as list of tuples (rows). Assign the column names to the rows and, thus, create a list of dictionaries. Each dictionary assigns the column names to the respective data values (Listing 2-10).

```
## Data
column_names = ['name', 'salary', 'job']
db_rows = [('Alice', 180000, 'data scientist'),
           ('Bob', 99000, 'mid-level manager'),
           ('Frank', 87000, 'CEO')]

## One-Liner
db = [dict(zip(column_names, row)) for row in db_rows]
```

```
## Result
print(db)
```

Listing 2-10: One-liner solution to apply a database format to a list of tuples

What's the printed format of the database db?

How It Works

You create the list by using list comprehension (see "Using List Comprehension to Find Top Earners" on page 18 for more on expression + context). The context consists of a tuple of every row in the variable db_rows. The expression zip(column_names, row) zips together the schema and each row. For example, the first element created by the list comprehension would be zip(['name', 'salary', 'job'], ('Alice', 180000, 'data scientist')), which results in a zip object that, after conversion to a list, is in the form [('name', 'Alice'), ('salary', 180000), ('job', 'data scientist')]. The elements are in (*key, value*) form so you can convert it into a dictionary by using the converter function dict() to arrive at the required database format.

NOTE *The zip() function doesn't care that one input is a list and the other is a tuple. The function requires only that the input is an iterable (and both lists and tuples are iterables).*

Here's the output of the one-liner code snippet:

```
## Result
print(db)
'''
[{'name': 'Alice', 'salary': 180000, 'job': 'data scientist'},
{'name': 'Bob', 'salary': 99000, 'job': 'mid-level manager'},
{'name': 'Frank', 'salary': 87000, 'job': 'CEO'}]
'''
```

Every data item is now associated with its name in a list of dictionaries. You've learned how to use the zip() function effectively.

Summary

In this chapter, you've mastered list comprehensions, file input, the functions lambda, map(), and zip(), the all() quantifier, slicing, and basic list arithmetic. You've also learned how to use and manipulate data structures to solve various day-to-day problems.

Converting data structures back and forth easily is a skill with a profound impact on your coding productivity. Rest assured that your programming productivity will soar as you increase your ability to quickly manipulate data. Small processing tasks like the ones you've seen in this chapter contribute significantly to the common "death by a thousand cuts": the overwhelming harm that performing many small tasks has on your overall productivity. By using the Python tricks, functions, and features introduced in this chapter, you've obtained effective protection against those thousand cuts. Speaking metaphorically, the newly acquired tools help you recover from each cut much faster.

In the next chapter, you'll improve your data science skills even further by diving into a new set of tools provided by the NumPy library for numerical computations in Python.

SOLUTION TO EXERCISE 2-1

Here's how to use list comprehension instead of the map() function to achieve the same problem of filtering out all lines that contain the string 'anonymous'. In this case, I even recommend using the faster and cleaner list comprehension feature.

```
mark = [(True, s) if 'anonymous' in s else (False, s) for s in txt]
```

3

DATA SCIENCE

The ability to analyze real-world data is one of the most sought-after skills in the 21st century. With the help of powerful hardware capabilities, algorithms, and ubiquitous sensing, data scientists create meaning from massive-scale raw data of weather statistics, financial transactions, customer behavior, and so much else. The largest companies in the world today—Google, Facebook, Apple, and Amazon—are essentially huge data-processing entities, with data at the heart of their business models.

This chapter equips you with the skills to process and analyze numerical data by using Python's library for numerical calculations, *NumPy*. I'll give you 10 practical problems and explain how to solve them in a single line of NumPy code. Because NumPy is the basis of many high-level libraries for data science and machine learning (Pandas, scikit-learn, and TensorFlow, for example), carefully studying this chapter will increase your market value in today's data-driven economy. So, give me your full attention!

Basic Two-Dimensional Array Arithmetic

Here you'll solve a day-to-day accounting task in a single line of code. I'll introduce some elementary functionalities of NumPy, Python's wildly important library for numerical computations and data science.

The Basics

At the heart of the NumPy library are *NumPy arrays*, which hold the data you want to manipulate, analyze, and visualize. Many higher-level data science libraries like Pandas build upon NumPy arrays, either implicitly or explicitly.

NumPy arrays are similar to Python lists but with some added bonuses. First, NumPy arrays have a smaller memory footprint and are faster in most instances. Second, NumPy arrays are more convenient when accessing more than two axes, known as *multidimensional* data (multidimensional lists are difficult to access and modify). Because a NumPy array can consist of more than one axis, we think of arrays in terms of *dimensions*: an array with two axes is a two-dimensional array. Third, NumPy arrays have more powerful access functionality, such as broadcasting, which you'll learn more about in this chapter.

Listing 3-1 exemplifies how to create one-dimensional, two-dimensional, and three-dimensional NumPy arrays.

```
import numpy as np


# Creating a 1D array from a list
a = np.array([1, 2, 3])
print(a)
"""
[1 2 3]
"""



# Creating a 2D array from a list of lists
b = np.array([[1, 2],
              [3, 4]])
print(b)
"""
[[1 2]
 [3 4]]
"""



# Creating a 3D array from a list of lists of lists
c = np.array([[[1, 2], [3, 4]],
              [[5, 6], [7, 8]]])
print(c)
"""
[[[1 2]
  [3 4]]
```

```
[[5 6]
 [7 8]]]
"""
```

Listing 3-1: Creating 1D, 2D, and 3D arrays in NumPy

You start by importing the NumPy library into the namespace by using the de facto standard name for the library: np. After importing the library, you create a NumPy array by passing a standard Python list as an argument to the function np.array(). A one-dimensional array corresponds to a simple list of numerical values (in fact, NumPy arrays can contain other data types too, but we'll focus on numbers here). A two-dimensional array corresponds to a nested *list of lists* of numerical values. A three-dimensional array corresponds to a nested *list of lists of lists* of numerical values. The number of opening and closing brackets gives you the dimensionality of the NumPy array.

NumPy arrays are more powerful than built-in Python lists. For instance, you can calculate basic arithmetic operators +, -, *, and / on two NumPy arrays. These *element-wise operations* combine two arrays a and b (for example, adding them together with the + operator) by combining each element of array a with the corresponding element of array b. In other words, an element-wise operation aggregates two elements that are at the same positions in the arrays a and b. Listing 3-2 shows examples of basic arithmetic operations on two-dimensional arrays.

```
import numpy as np


a = np.array([[1, 0, 0],
              [1, 1, 1],
              [2, 0, 0]])

b = np.array([[1, 1, 1],
              [1, 1, 2],
              [1, 1, 2]])


print(a + b)
"""
[[2 1 1]
 [2 2 3]
 [3 1 2]]
"""


print(a - b)
"""
[[ 0 -1 -1]
 [ 0  0 -1]
 [ 1 -1 -2]]
"""


print(a * b)
"""
```

```
[[1 0 0]
 [1 1 2]
 [2 0 0]]
"""

print(a / b)
"""
[[1.  0.  0. ]
 [1.  1.  0.5]
 [2.  0.  0. ]]
"""
```

Listing 3-2: Basic arithmetic array operations

NOTE   *When you apply NumPy operators to integer arrays, they try to generate integer arrays as results too. Only when dividing two integer arrays by using the division operator, a / b, will the result be a float array. This is indicated by the decimal points: 1., 0., and 0.5.*

If you look closely, you'll find that each operation combines two corresponding NumPy arrays element-wise. When adding two arrays, the result is a new array: each new value is the sum of the corresponding value from the first and the second array. The same holds true when you use subtraction, multiplication, and division, as shown.

NumPy provides a lot more capabilities for manipulating arrays, including the np.max() function, which calculates the *maximum* value of all values in a NumPy array. The np.min() function calculates the *minimum* value of all values in a NumPy array. The np.average() function calculates the *average* value of all values in a NumPy array.

Listing 3-3 gives an example of these three operations.

```
import numpy as np


a = np.array([[1, 0, 0],
              [1, 1, 1],
              [2, 0, 0]])

print(np.max(a))
# 2

print(np.min(a))
# 0

print(np.average(a))
# 0.6666666666666666
```

Listing 3-3: Calculating the maximum, minimum, and average value of a NumPy array

The maximum value of all values in the NumPy array is 2, the minimum value is 0, and the average is (1 + 0 + 0 + 1 + 1 + 1 + 2 + 0 + 0) / 9 = 2/3. NumPy has many more powerful tools, but this is already enough to solve the following problem: how do we find the maximum after-tax income in a group of people, given their yearly salary and tax rates?

The Code

Let's tackle this problem by using the salary data of Alice, Bob, and Tim. It seems like Bob has enjoyed the highest salary in the last three years. But is he actually bringing home the most money, considering the individual tax rates of our three friends? Take a look at Listing 3-4.

```
## Dependencies
import numpy as np


## Data: yearly salary in ($1000) [2017, 2018, 2019]
alice = [99, 101, 103]
bob = [110, 108, 105]
tim = [90, 88, 85]

salaries = np.array([alice, bob, tim])
taxation = np.array([[0.2, 0.25, 0.22],
                     [0.4, 0.5, 0.5],
                     [0.1, 0.2, 0.1]])


## One-liner
max_income = np.max(salaries - salaries * taxation)


## Result
print(max_income)
```

Listing 3-4: One-liner solution using basic array arithmetic

Take a guess: what's the output of this code?

How It Works

After importing the NumPy library, you put the data into a two-dimensional NumPy array with three rows (one row for each person: Alice, Bob, and Tim) and three columns (one column for each year: 2017, 2018, and 2019). You have two two-dimensional arrays: salaries holds the yearly incomes, and taxation holds the taxation rates for each person and year.

To calculate the after-tax income, you need to deduct the tax (as a dollar amount) from the gross income stored in the array salaries. For this, you use the overloaded NumPy operators - and *, which perform element-wise computations on the NumPy arrays.

The element-wise multiplication of two multidimensional arrays is called the *Hadamard product*.

Listing 3-5 shows how the NumPy array looks after deducting the taxes from the gross incomes.

```
print(salaries - salaries * taxation)
"""
[[79.2  75.75 80.34]
 [66.   54.   52.5 ]
 [81.   70.4  76.5 ]]
"""
```

Listing 3-5: Basic array arithmetic

Here, you can see that Bob's large income is significantly reduced after paying 40 percent and 50 percent tax rates, shown in the second row.

The code snippet prints the maximum value of this resulting array. The `np.max()` function simply finds the maximum value in the array, which you store in `max_income`. Thus, the maximum value is Tim's $90,000 income in 2017, which is taxed at only 10 percent—the result of the one-liner is `81.` (again, the dot indicates the float data type).

You've used NumPy's basic element-wise array arithmetic to analyze the taxation rates of a group of people. Let's use the same example data set in applying intermediate NumPy concepts such as slicing and broadcasting.

Working with NumPy Arrays: Slicing, Broadcasting, and Array Types

This one-liner demonstrates the power of three interesting NumPy features: slicing, broadcasting, and array types. Our data is an array of multiple professions and salaries. You'll use the three concepts in combination to increase the salaries of just the data scientists by 10 percent every other year.

The Basics

The crux of our problem is being able to change specific values in a NumPy array with many rows. You want to change every other value for one single row. Let's explore the basics you need to know to be able to solve this problem.

Slicing and Indexing

Indexing and slicing in NumPy are similar to indexing and slicing in Python (see Chapter 2): you can access elements of a one-dimensional array by using the bracket operation [] to specify the index or index range. For example, the indexing operation x[3] returns the fourth element of the NumPy array x (because you access the first element with index 0).

You can also use indexing for a multidimensional array by specifying the index for each dimension independently and using comma-separated indices to access the different dimensions. For example, the indexing operation y[0,1,2] would access the first element of the first axis, the second element of the second axis, and the third element of the third axis. Note that this syntax would be invalid for multidimensional Python lists.

Let's move on to *slicing* in NumPy. Study the examples in Listing 3-6 to master one-dimensional slicing in NumPy, and feel free to go back to

Chapter 2 to revisit basic Python slicing if you have difficulties understanding these examples.

```python
import numpy as np


a = np.array([55, 56, 57, 58, 59, 60, 61])
print(a)
# [55 56 57 58 59 60 61]

print(a[:])
# [55 56 57 58 59 60 61]

print(a[2:])
# [57 58 59 60 61]

print(a[1:4])
# [56 57 58]

print(a[2:-2])
# [57 58 59]

print(a[::2])
# [55 57 59 61]

print(a[1::2])
# [56 58 60]

print(a[::-1])
# [61 60 59 58 57 56 55]

print(a[:1:-2])
# [61 59 57]

print(a[-1:1:-2])
# [61 59 57]
```

Listing 3-6: One-dimensional slicing examples

The next step is to fully understand multidimensional slicing. Much as for indexing, you apply one-dimensional slicing separately for each axis (comma-separated) to select a range of elements along this axis. Take your time to thoroughly understand the examples in Listing 3-7.

```python
import numpy as np


a = np.array([[0, 1, 2, 3],
              [4, 5, 6, 7],
              [8, 9, 10, 11],
              [12, 13, 14, 15]])

print(a[:, 2])
# Third col: [ 2  6 10 14]
```

```
print(a[1, :])
# Second row: [4 5 6 7]

print(a[1, ::2])
# Second row, every other element: [4 6]

print(a[:, :-1])
# All columns except last:
# [[ 0  1  2]
# [ 4  5  6]
# [ 8  9 10]
# [12 13 14]]

print(a[:-2])
# Same as a[:-2, :]
# [[ 0  1  2  3]
# [ 4  5  6  7]]
```

Listing 3-7: Multidimensional slicing examples

Study Listing 3-7 until you understand multidimensional slicing. You can perform two-dimensional slicing by using the syntax a[*slice1, slice2*]. For any additional dimension, add a comma-separated slicing operation (using the start:stop or start:stop:step slicing operators). Each slice selects an independent subsequence of the elements in its respective dimension. If you understand this basic idea, going from one-dimensional to multidimensional slicing is trivial.

Broadcasting

Broadcasting describes the automatic process of bringing two NumPy arrays into the same shape so that you can apply certain element-wise operations (see "Slicing and Indexing" on page 46). Broadcasting is closely related to the *shape attribute* of NumPy arrays, which in turn is closely related to the concept of axes. So, let's dive into axes, shapes, and broadcasting next.

Each array comprises several *axes*, one for each dimension (Listing 3-8).

```
import numpy as np

a = np.array([1, 2, 3, 4])
print(a.ndim)
# 1

b = np.array([[2, 1, 2], [3, 2, 3], [4, 3, 4]])
print(b.ndim)
# 2

c = np.array([[[1, 2, 3], [2, 3, 4], [3, 4, 5]],
              [[1, 2, 4], [2, 3, 5], [3, 4, 6]]])
print(c.ndim)
# 3
```

Listing 3-8: Axes and dimensionality of three NumPy arrays

Here, you can see three arrays: a, b, and c. The array attribute ndim stores the number of axes of this particular array. You simply print it to the shell for each array. Array a is one-dimensional, array b is two-dimensional, and array c is three-dimensional. Every array has an associated shape attribute, a tuple that gives you the number of elements in each axis. For a two-dimensional array, there are two values in the tuple: the number of rows and the number of columns. For higher-dimensional arrays, the i-th tuple value specifies the number of elements of the i-th axis. The number of tuple elements is therefore the dimensionality of the NumPy array.

NOTE *If you increase the dimensionality of an array (for example, you move from 2D to 3D arrays), the new axis becomes axis 0, and the i-th axis of the low-dimensional array becomes the $(i + 1)$-th axis of the high-dimensional array.*

Listing 3-9 gives the shape attributes of the same arrays from Listing 3-8.

```
import numpy as np


a = np.array([1, 2, 3, 4])
print(a)
"""
[1 2 3 4]
"""

print(a.shape)
# (4,)

b = np.array([[2, 1, 2], [3, 2, 3], [4, 3, 4]])
print(b)
"""
[[2 1 2]
 [3 2 3]
 [4 3 4]]
"""

print(b.shape)
# (3, 3)

c = np.array([[[1, 2, 3], [2, 3, 4], [3, 4, 5]],
             [[1, 2, 4], [2, 3, 5], [3, 4, 6]]])
print(c)
"""
[[[1 2 3]
  [2 3 4]
  [3 4 5]]

 [[1 2 4]
  [2 3 5]
  [3 4 6]]]
"""

print(c.shape)
# (2, 3, 3)
```

Listing 3-9: The shape property of 1D, 2D, and 3D NumPy arrays

Here, you can see that the shape attributes contain much more information than the ndim attributes. Every shape attribute is a tuple with the number of elements along each axis:

- Array a is one-dimensional, so the shape tuple has only a single element that represents the number of columns (four elements).

- Array b is two-dimensional, so the shape tuple has two elements that enumerate the number of rows and columns.

- Array c is three-dimensional, so the shape tuple has three elements—one for each axis. Axis 0 has two elements (each element is a two-dimensional array), axis 1 has three elements (each is a one-dimensional array), and axis 2 has three elements (each is an integer value).

Now that you understand the shape attribute, it'll be easier to grasp the general idea of broadcasting: bringing two arrays into the same shape by rearranging the data. Let's see how broadcasting works. Broadcasting automatically fixes element-wise operations of NumPy arrays with different shapes. For example, the multiplication operator * usually performs element-wise multiplication when applied to NumPy arrays. But what happens if the left and right data don't match (say, the left operator is a NumPy array, while the right is a float value)? In this case, rather than throwing an error, NumPy automatically creates a new array from the right-side data. The new array has the same size and dimensionality as the array on the left and contains the same float values.

Broadcasting, therefore, is the act of converting a low-dimensional array into a higher-dimensional array to perform element-wise operations.

Homogenous Values

NumPy arrays are *homogeneous*, meaning all values have the same type. Here is a non-exclusive list of possible array data types:

bool   The Boolean data type in Python (1 byte)

int   The integer data type in Python (default size: 4 or 8 bytes)

float   The float data type in Python (default size: 8 bytes)

complex   The complex data type in Python (default size: 16 bytes)

np.int8   An integer data type (1 byte)

np.int16   An integer data type (2 bytes)

np.int32   An integer data type (4 bytes)

np.int64   An integer data type (8 bytes)

np.float16   A float data type (2 bytes)

np.float32   A float data type (4 bytes)

np.float64   A float data type (8 bytes)

Listing 3-10 shows how to create NumPy arrays with different types.

```
import numpy as np

a = np.array([1, 2, 3, 4], dtype=np.int16)
print(a) # [1 2 3 4]
print(a.dtype) # int16

b = np.array([1, 2, 3, 4], dtype=np.float64)
print(b) # [1. 2. 3. 4.]
print(b.dtype) # float64
```

Listing 3-10: NumPy arrays with different types

This code has two arrays, a and b. The first array a is of data type np.int16. The numbers are of type integer (there is no "dot" after the number). Specifically, when printing out the dtype property of array a, you get the result int16.

The second array b is of data type float64. So even if you create the array based on a list of integers, NumPy will convert the array type to np.float64.

There are two important takeaways here: NumPy gives you control over the data type, and the data type of a NumPy array is homogeneous.

The Code

You have data for a variety of professions, and you want to increase the salaries of just the data scientists by 10 percent every other year. Listing 3-11 presents the code.

```
## Dependencies
import numpy as np


## Data: yearly salary in ($1000) [2025, 2026, 2027]
dataScientist =     [130, 132, 137]
productManager =    [127, 140, 145]
designer =          [118, 118, 127]
softwareEngineer =  [129, 131, 137]

employees = np.array([dataScientist,
                      productManager,
                      designer,
                      softwareEngineer])


## One-liner
employees[0,::2] = employees[0,::2] * 1.1


## Result
print(employees)
```

Listing 3-11: One-liner solution using slicing and slice assignments

Take a minute and think about the output of this code snippet. What would you expect to change? What's the data type of the resulting array? What is the output of this code?

How It Works

The code snippet places you in the year 2024. First, you create a NumPy array with each row holding the expected yearly salaries of one professional (data scientist, product manager, designer, or software engineer). Each column gives the respective future years' salaries in 2025, 2026, and 2027. The resulting NumPy array has four rows and three columns.

You have funds available to reinforce the most important professionals in the company. You believe in the future of data science, so you decide to reward the hidden heroes of your company: the data scientists. You need to update the NumPy array so that only the data scientists' salaries increase by 10 percent every other year (non-cumulatively), starting from the year 2025.

You develop the following beautiful one-liner:

```
employees[0,::2] = employees[0,::2] * 1.1
```

It looks simple and clean, and provides the following output:

```
[[143 132 150]
 [127 140 145]
 [118 118 127]
 [129 131 137]]
```

Though simple, your one-liner has three interesting and advanced concepts at play.

Slicing

First, you use the concept of *slices* and *slice assignment*. In the example, you use slicing to get every other value of the first row from the NumPy array employees. Then, you perform some modifications and update every other value of the first row by using slice assignment. Slice assignment uses the same syntax as slicing, with one crucial difference: you select the slice on the left of the assignment. These elements will be replaced by the elements specified on the right of the assignment operation. In the code snippet, you replace the content of the first row in the NumPy array with the updated salary data.

Broadcasting

Second, you use broadcasting, which automatically fixes element-wise operations of NumPy arrays with different shapes. In the one-liner, the left operator is a NumPy array, while the right is a float value. Again, NumPy automatically creates a new array, making it the same size and dimensionality as the array on the left and filling it, conceptually, with copies of the float value. In reality, NumPy performs a computation that looks more like the following:

```
np.array([130 137]) * np.array([1.1, 1.1])
```

Array Types

Third, you may have realized that the resulting data type is not float but integer, even if you are performing floating-point arithmetic. When you create the array, NumPy realizes it contains only integer values, and so assumes it to be an integer array. Any operation you perform on the integer array won't change the data type, and NumPy will round down to integer values. Again, you can access the array's type by using the dtype property:

```
print(employees.dtype)
# int32
employees[0,::2] = employees[0,::2] * 1.1
print(employees.dtype)
# int32
```

In summary, you've learned about slicing, slice assignments, broadcasting, and NumPy array types—quite an accomplishment in a one-liner code snippet. Let's build upon that by solving a small data science problem with real-world impact: detecting outliers in pollution measurements of various cities.

Conditional Array Search, Filtering, and Broadcasting to Detect Outliers

In this one-liner, you'll explore air-quality data of cities. Specifically, given a two-dimensional NumPy array with pollution measurements (columns) for multiple cities (rows), you'll find the cities that have above-average pollution measurements. The skills you'll acquire by reading this section are important in finding outliers in data sets.

The Basics

The Air Quality Index (AQI) measures the danger of adverse health effects and is commonly used to compare differences in cities' air quality. In this one-liner, you're going to look at the AQI of four cities: Hong Kong, New York, Berlin, and Montreal.

The one-liner finds above-average polluted cities, defined as cities that have a peak AQI value that is above the overall average among all the measurements of all cities.

An important element of our solution will be to find elements in a NumPy array that meet a certain condition. This is a common problem in data science you'll use very often.

So, let's explore how to find array elements that meet a specific condition. NumPy offers the function nonzero() that finds indices of elements in an array that are, well, not equal to zero. Listing 3-12 gives an example.

```
import numpy as np

X = np.array([[1, 0, 0],
              [0, 2, 2],
              [3, 0, 0]])

print(np.nonzero(X))
```

Listing 3-12: The nonzero function

The result is a tuple of two NumPy arrays:

```
(array([0, 1, 1, 2], dtype=int64), array([0, 1, 2, 0], dtype=int64)).
```

The first array gives the row indices, and the second gives the column indices of the nonzero elements. There are four nonzero elements in the two-dimensional array: 1, 2, 2, and 3, found at positions X[0,0], X[1,1], X[1,2], and X[2,0] in the original array.

Now, how can you use nonzero() to find elements that meet a certain condition in your array? You'll use another great NumPy feature: Boolean array operations with broadcasting (see Listing 3-13)!

```
import numpy as np

X = np.array([[1, 0, 0],
              [0, 2, 2],
              [3, 0, 0]])

print(X == 2)
"""
[[False False False]
 [False  True  True]
 [False False False]]
"""
```

Listing 3-13: Broadcasting and element-wise Boolean operators in NumPy

Broadcasting occurs as the integer value 2 is copied (conceptually) into a new array with the same shape as the array. NumPy then performs an element-wise comparison of each integer against the value 2 and returns the resulting Boolean array.

In our main code, you'll combine the nonzero() and Boolean array operation features to find elements that meet a certain condition.

The Code

In Listing 3-14, you're finding cities with above-average pollution peaks from a set of data.

```
## Dependencies
import numpy as np

## Data: air quality index AQI data (row = city)
X = np.array(
    [[ 42, 40, 41, 43, 44, 43 ], # Hong Kong
     [ 30, 31, 29, 29, 29, 30 ], # New York
     [ 8, 13, 31, 11, 11, 9 ], # Berlin
     [ 11, 11, 12, 13, 11, 12 ]]) # Montreal

cities = np.array(["Hong Kong", "New York", "Berlin", "Montreal"])

## One-liner
polluted = set(cities[np.nonzero(X > np.average(X))[0]])

## Result
print(polluted)
```

Listing 3-14: One-liner solution using broadcasting, Boolean operators, and selective indexing

See if you can determine what the output of this code would be.

How It Works

The data array X contains four rows (one row for each city) and six columns (one column for each measurement unit—in this case, days). The string array cities contains the four names of the cities in the order they occur in the data array.

Here is the one-liner that finds the cities with above-average observed AQI values:

```
## One-liner
polluted = set(cities[np.nonzero(X > np.average(X))[0]])
```

You first need to understand the parts before you can understand the whole. To better understand the one-liner, let's deconstruct it by starting from within. At the heart of the one-liner is the Boolean array operation (see Listing 3-15).

```
print(X > np.average(X))
"""
[[ True  True  True  True  True  True]
 [ True  True  True  True  True  True]
 [False False  True False False False]
 [False False False False False False]]
"""
```

Listing 3-15: Boolean array operation using broadcasting

You use a Boolean expression to bring both operands to the same shape with broadcasting. You use the function np.average() to compute the average AQI value of all NumPy array elements. The Boolean expression then performs an element-wise comparison to come up with a Boolean array that contains True if the respective measurement observed is an above-average AQI value.

By generating this Boolean array, you know precisely which elements satisfy the condition of being above-average and which elements don't.

Recall that Python's True value is represented by the integer 1, and False is represented by 0. In fact, the True and False objects are of type bool, which is a subclass of int. Thus, every Boolean value is also an integer value. With this, you can use the function nonzero() to find all row and column indices that meet the condition, like so:

```
print(np.nonzero(X > np.average(X)))
"""
(array([0, 0, 0, 0, 0, 0, 1, 1, 1, 1, 1, 1, 2], dtype=int64),
array([0, 1, 2, 3, 4, 5, 0, 1, 2, 3, 4, 5, 2], dtype=int64))
"""
```

You have two tuples, the first giving the row indices of nonzero elements, and the second giving their respective column indices.

We're looking only for the names of the cities with above-average AQI values, and nothing else, so you need just the row indices. You can use these row indices to extract the string names from our string array by using *advanced indexing*, an indexing technique that allows you to define a sequence of array indices without requiring it to be a continuous slice. This way, you can access arbitrary elements from a given NumPy array by specifying either a sequence of integers (the indices to be selected) or a sequence of Booleans (to select the specific indices where the corresponding Boolean value is True):

```
print(cities[np.nonzero(X > np.average(X))[0]])
"""
['Hong Kong' 'Hong Kong' 'Hong Kong' 'Hong Kong' 'Hong Kong' 'Hong Kong'
 'New York' 'New York' 'New York' 'New York' 'New York' 'New York'
 'Berlin']
"""
```

You'll notice many duplicates in the resulting sequence of strings, because Hong Kong and New York have multiple above-average AQI measurements.

Now, there is only one thing left to do: remove duplicates. You'll do this by converting the sequence to a Python set, which is by default duplicate-free, giving a succinct summary of all city names with pollution that exceeded the average AQI values.

In summary, you learned about using Boolean expressions on NumPy arrays (using broadcasting again) and the nonzero() function to find rows or columns that satisfy certain conditions. After saving the environment in this one-liner, let's move on and analyze influencers in social media.

Boolean Indexing to Filter Two-Dimensional Arrays

Here you'll strengthen your knowledge of array indexing and broadcasting by pulling Instagram users with more than 100 million followers from a small data set. In particular, given a two-dimensional array of influencers (rows), with a first column that defines the influencer's name as a string and a second column that defines the influencer's follower count, you'll find all influencer names with more than 100 million followers!

The Basics

NumPy arrays enrich the basic list data type with additional functionality such as multidimensional slicing and multidimensional indexing. Have a look at the code snippet in Listing 3-16.

```
import numpy as np


a = np.array([[1, 2, 3],
              [4, 5, 6],
              [7, 8, 9]])

indices = np.array([[False, False, True],
                    [False, False, False],
                    [True, True, False]])

print(a[indices])
# [3 7 8]
```

Listing 3-16: Selective (Boolean) indexing in NumPy

You create two arrays: a contains two-dimensional numerical data (think of it as the *data array*), and indices contains Boolean values (think of it as the *indexing array*). A great feature of NumPy is that you can use the Boolean array for fine-grained access to the data array. In plain English, you create a new array containing only those elements of the data array a for which the indexing array indices contains True values at the respective array positions. For example, if indices[i,j]==True, the new array contains the value a[i,j]. Similarly, if indices[i,j]==False, the new array does not contain the value a[i,j]. Thus, the resulting array contains the three values 3, 7, and 8.

In the following one-liner, you are going to use this feature for a toy analysis of a social network.

The Code

In Listing 3-17, you'll find the names of the Instagram superstars with more than 100 million followers!

```
## Dependencies
import numpy as np


## Data: popular Instagram accounts (millions followers)
inst = np.array([[232, "@instagram"],
                 [133, "@selenagomez"],
                 [59,  "@victoriassecret"],
                 [120, "@cristiano"],
                 [111, "@beyonce"],
                 [76,  "@nike"]])


## One-liner
superstars = inst[inst[:,0].astype(float) > 100, 1]


## Results
print(superstars)
```

Listing 3-17: One-liner solution using slicing, array types, and Boolean operators

As usual, see if you can compute the result of this one-liner in your head before reading through the explanation.

How It Works

The data consists of a two-dimensional array, inst, and each row represents an Instagram influencer. The first column states their number of followers (in millions), and the second column states their Instagram name. From this data, you want to pull the names of the Instagram influencers with more than 100 million followers.

There are many ways to solve this in one line. The following approach is the easiest one:

```
## One-liner
superstars = inst[inst[:,0].astype(float) > 100, 1]
```

Let's deconstruct this one-liner step by step. The inner expression calculates a Boolean value that says whether each influencer has more than 100 million followers:

```
print(inst[:,0].astype(float) > 100)
# [ True  True False  True  True False]
```

The first column contains the number of followers, so you use slicing to access this data; inst[:,0] returns all rows in just the first column. However, because the data array contains mixed data types (integers and strings), NumPy automatically assigns a non-numerical data type to the array. The reason is that a numerical data type would not be able to capture the string data, so NumPy converts the data to a type that can represent all data in the array (string and numerical). You need to perform numerical comparisons on the first column of the data array to check whether each value is larger than 100, so you first convert the resulting array into a float type by using .astype(float).

Next, you check whether the values in the float type NumPy array are each larger than the integer value 100. Here, NumPy again uses broadcasting to automatically bring the two operands into the same shape so it can do the comparison element-wise. The result is an array of Boolean values that shows that four influencers have more than 100 million followers.

You now take this Boolean array (also called a *mask index array*) to select the influencers with more than 100 million followers (the rows) by using Boolean indexing:

```
inst[inst[:,0].astype(float) > 100, 1]
```

Because you are interested only in the names of these influencers, you select the second column as the final result and store it in the superstars variable.

The influencers from our data set with more than 100 million Instagram followers are as follows:

```
# ['@instagram' '@selenagomez' '@cristiano' '@beyonce']
```

In summary, you've applied NumPy concepts such as slicing, broadcasting, Boolean indexing, and data type conversion to a small data science problem in social media analysis. Next, you'll learn about a new application scenario in the Internet of Things.

Broadcasting, Slice Assignment, and Reshaping to Clean Every i-th Array Element

Real-world data is seldom clean and may contain errors or missing values for a huge variety of reasons, including damaged or faulty sensors. In this section, you'll learn about how to handle small cleaning tasks to eliminate erroneous data points.

The Basics

Say you've installed a temperature sensor in your garden to measure temperature data over many weeks. Every Sunday, you bring the temperature sensor in from the garden to digitize the sensor values. You're aware that the Sunday sensor values are therefore faulty because for part of the day they measure the temperature in your home instead of outside.

You want to clean your data by replacing every Sunday sensor value with the average sensor value of the previous seven days (you include the Sunday value in the average computation because it's not entirely faulty). Before diving into the code, let's explore the most important concepts you need as a basic understanding.

Slice Assignment

With NumPy's slice assignment feature (see "Working with NumPy Arrays: Slicing, Broadcasting, and Array Types" on page 46), you specify the values you want to replace on the left of the equation, and the values to replace them with on the right-hand side of the equation. Listing 3-18 provides an example in case you need a small recap.

```
import numpy as np


a = np.array([4] * 16)
print(a)
# [4 4 4 4 4 4 4 4 4 4 4 4 4 4 4 4]

a[1::] = [42] * 15
print(a)
# [ 4 42 42 42 42 42 42 42 42 42 42 42 42 42 42 42]
```

Listing 3-18: Simple Python list creation and slice assignment

The code snippet creates an array containing the value 4 sixteen times. You use slice assignment to replace the last fifteen values with the value 42. Recall that the notation a[start:stop:step] selects the sequence starting at index start, ending at index stop (exclusive), and considering only every step-th sequence element. If no arguments are specified, NumPy assumes default values. The notation a[1::] replaces all sequence elements but the first one. Listing 3-19 shows how to use slice assignment in combination with a feature you've already seen multiple times.

```
import numpy as np

a = np.array([4] * 16)

a[1:8:2] = 16
print(a)
# [ 4 16  4 16  4 16  4 16  4  4  4  4  4  4  4  4]
```

Listing 3-19: Slice assignment in NumPy

Here you replace every other value between index 1 and 8 (exclusive). You can see that you need to specify only a single value, 16, to replace the selected elements, because of—you guessed it—*broadcasting*! The right side of the equation is automatically transformed into a NumPy array that is the same shape as the left array.

Reshaping

Before diving into the one-liner, you need to learn about an important NumPy function: the x.reshape((a,b)) function that transforms the NumPy array x into a new NumPy array with a rows and b columns (with shape (a,b)). Here's an example:

```
a = np.array([1, 2, 3, 4, 5, 6])
print(a.reshape((2, 3)))
'''

[[1 2 3]
 [4 5 6]]
'''
```

If the number of columns is unambiguous, you can also let NumPy do the work of figuring out the number of columns automatically. Let's say you want to reshape an array with six elements into a two-dimensional array with two rows. NumPy can now figure out that it needs three columns to match the six elements in the original array. Here's an example:

```
a = np.array([1, 2, 3, 4, 5, 6])
print(a.reshape((2, -1)))
'''

[[1 2 3]
 [4 5 6]]
'''
```

The shape value -1 for the column argument indicates that NumPy should replace it with the correct number of columns (which is three in this case).

The Axis Argument

Finally, let's consider the following code snippet that introduces the axis argument. Here is an array solar_x that contains daily stock prices of Elon

Musk's SolarX company. We want to calculate the average stock prices in the mornings, middays, and evenings. How can we achieve this?

```
import numpy as np


# daily stock prices
# [morning, midday, evening]
solar_x = np.array(
    [[1, 2, 3], # today
     [2, 2, 5]]) # yesterday

# midday - weighted average
print(np.average(solar_x, axis=0))
# [1.5 2.  4. ]
```

The array solar_x consists of stock prices of the SolarX company. It has two rows (one for each day) and three columns (one for each stock price). Say we want to calculate the average stock price in the mornings, the middays, and the evenings. Roughly speaking, we want to collapse together all values in each column by averaging them. In other words, we calculate the average along axis 0. This is exactly what the keyword argument axis=0 is doing.

The Code

This is everything you need to know to solve the following problem (Listing 3-20): given an array of temperature values, replace every seventh temperature value with the average of the last seven days (including the seventh day's temperature value).

```
## Dependencies
import numpy as np

## Sensor data (Mo, Tu, We, Th, Fr, Sa, Su)
tmp = np.array([1, 2, 3, 4, 3, 4, 4,
                5, 3, 3, 4, 3, 4, 6,
                6, 5, 5, 5, 4, 5, 5])


## One-liner
tmp[6::7] = np.average(tmp.reshape((-1,7)), axis=1)


## Result
print(tmp)
```

Listing 3-20: One-liner solution using the average and reshape operators, slice assignments, and the axis argument

Can you calculate the output of this code snippet?

How It Works

The data arrives in the shape of a one-dimensional array of sensor values.

First, you create the data array `tmp` with a one-dimensional sequence of sensor values. In every line, you define all seven sensor values for seven days of the week.

Second, you use slice assignment to replace all the Sunday values of this array. Because Sunday is the seventh day, you use the expression `tmp[6::7]` to select the respective Sunday values, starting from the seventh element in the original array `tmp`.

Third, we *reshape* the one-dimensional sensor array into a two-dimensional array with seven columns and three rows, which makes it easier to calculate the weekly average temperature value to replace the Sunday data. Because of the reshaping, you can now merge all seven values of each row into a single average value. To reshape the array, you pass the tuple values -1 and 7 to `tmp.reshape()`, which tells NumPy that the number of rows (*axis 0*) should be selected automatically. Roughly speaking, you specify seven columns, and NumPy creates an array with however many rows are needed to satisfy our condition of seven columns. In our case, it results in the following array after reshaping:

```
print(tmp.reshape((-1,7)))
"""
[[1 2 3 4 3 4 4]
 [5 3 3 4 3 4 6]
 [6 5 5 5 4 5 5]]
"""
```

You have one row per week and one column per weekday.

Now you calculate the seven-day average by collapsing every row into a single average value by using the `np.average()` function with the axis argument: `axis=1` tells NumPy to collapse the second axis into a single average value. Note that the Sunday value is included in the average computation (see the problem formulation at the beginning of this section). This is the result of the right-hand side of the equation:

```
print(np.average(tmp.reshape((-1,7)), axis=1))
# [3. 4. 5.]
```

The goal of the one-liner is to replace the three Sunday temperature values. All other values should stay constant. Let's see whether you achieved this objective. After replacing all Sunday sensor values, you get the following final result of the one-liner:

```
# [1 2 3 4 3 4 3 5 3 3 4 3 4 4 6 5 5 5 4 5 5]
```

Note that you still have a one-dimensional NumPy array with all temperature sensor values. But now you've replaced the unrepresentative readings with more representative ones.

In summary, this one-liner is all about hammering down the concepts of array shapes and reshaping, and how to use the axis property for aggregator functions such as np.average(). While this application was rather specific, it will be useful in a range of situations. Next, you'll learn about a super general concept: sorting in NumPy.

When to Use the sort() Function and When to Use the argsort() Function in NumPy

Sorting is useful, even essential, in numerous situations. Say you search your bookshelf for *Python One-Liners*. It would be much easier to find the book if your bookshelf were alphabetically sorted by title.

This one-liner solution will show you how to use sorting in a single line of Python by using NumPy.

The Basics

Sorting is at the heart of more advanced applications such as commercial computing, process scheduling in operating systems (priority queues), and search algorithms. Fortunately, NumPy provides various sorting algorithms. The default is the popular *Quicksort* algorithm. In Chapter 6, you'll learn how to implement the Quicksort algorithm yourself. However, for this one-liner, you'll take a higher-level approach, viewing the sorting function as a black box into which you'll put a NumPy array to get out a sorted NumPy array.

Figure 3-1 shows the algorithm transforming an unsorted array into a sorted array. This is the purpose of NumPy's sort() function.

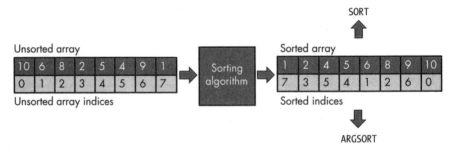

Figure 3-1: The difference between the sort() and argsort() functions

But often, it's also important to get the array of indices that would transform the unsorted array into a sorted array. For example, the unsorted array element 1 has index 7. Because the array element 1 is the first element of the sorted array, its index 7 is the first element of the sorted indices. This is what NumPy's argsort() function does: it creates a new array of the original index values after sorting (see the example in Figure 3-1). Roughly speaking, these indices would sort the elements in the original array. By using this array, you can reconstruct both the sorted and the original array.

Listing 3-21 demonstrates the use of sort() and argsort() in NumPy.

```
import numpy as np


a = np.array([10, 6, 8, 2, 5, 4, 9, 1])

print(np.sort(a))
# [ 1  2  4  5  6  8  9 10]

print(np.argsort(a))
# [7 3 5 4 1 2 6 0]
```

Listing 3-21: The sort() and argsort() functions in NumPy

You create an unsorted array a, sort it with np.sort(a), and get the original indices in their new sorted order with np.argsort(a). NumPy's sort() function is different from Python's sorted() function in that it can sort multi-dimensional arrays too!

Figure 3-2 shows two ways of sorting a two-dimensional array.

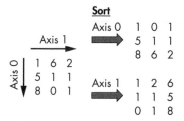

Figure 3-2: Sorting along an axis

The array has two axes: axis 0 (the rows) and axis 1 (the columns). You can sort along axis 0, known as *vertical sorting*, or along axis 1, known as *horizontal sorting*. In general, the axis keyword defines the direction along which you perform the NumPy operation. Listing 3-22 shows technically how to do this.

```
import numpy as np


a = np.array([[1, 6, 2],
              [5, 1, 1],
              [8, 0, 1]])

print(np.sort(a, axis=0))
"""

[[1 0 1]
 [5 1 1]
 [8 6 2]]
"""
```

```
print(np.sort(a, axis=1))
"""
[[1 2 6]
 [1 1 5]
 [0 1 8]]
"""
```

Listing 3-22: Sorting along an axis

The optional axis argument helps you sort the NumPy array along a fixed direction. First, you sort by columns, starting with the smallest value. Then you sort by rows. This is the main strength of NumPy's sort() function compared to Python's built-in sorted() function.

The Code

This one-liner will find the names of the top three students with the highest SAT scores. Note that you'll ask for the student names and not the sorted SAT scores. Have a look at the data and see if you can find the one-liner solution yourself. When you've had a go at that, take a look at Listing 3-23.

```
## Dependencies
import numpy as np


## Data: SAT scores for different students
sat_scores = np.array([1100, 1256, 1543, 1043, 989, 1412, 1343])
students = np.array(["John", "Bob", "Alice", "Joe", "Jane", "Frank", "Carl"])


## One-liner
top_3 = students[np.argsort(sat_scores)][:-4:-1]


## Result
print(top_3)
```

Listing 3-23: One-liner solution using the argsort() function and slicing with negative step size

As usual, try to figure out the output.

How It Works

Our initial data consists of the SAT scores of students as a one-dimensional data array, and another array with the corresponding names of the students. For example, John achieved a solid SAT score of 1100, while Frank achieved an excellent SAT score of 1412.

The task is to find the names of the three most successful students. You'll achieve this—not by simply sorting the SAT scores—but by running the `argsort()` function to get an array of the original indices in their new sorted positions.

Here is the output of the `argsort()` function on the SAT scores:

```
print(np.argsort(sat_scores))
# [4 3 0 1 6 5 2]
```

You need to retain the indexes because you need to be able to find the name of the student from the `students` array, which corresponds only to the original positions. Index 4 is at the first position of the output because Jane has the lowest SAT score, with 989 points. Note that both `sort()` and `argsort()` sort in an ascending manner, from lowest to highest values.

Now that you have sorted indices, you need to get the names of the respective students by indexing the `student` array:

```
print(students[np.argsort(sat_scores)])
# ['Jane' 'Joe' 'John' 'Bob' 'Carl' 'Frank' 'Alice']
```

This is a useful feature of the NumPy library: you can reorder a sequence by using advanced indexing. If you specify a sequence of indices, NumPy triggers advanced indexing and returns a new NumPy array with reordered elements as specified by your index sequence. For instance, the command `students[np.argsort(sat_scores)]` evaluates to `students[[4 3 0 1 6 5 2]]` so NumPy creates a new array as follows:

```
[students[4]  students[3]  students[0]  students[1]  students[6]  students[5]  students[2]]
```

From this, you know that Jane has the lowest SAT score, while Alice has the highest. The only thing left is to reverse the list and extract the top three students by using simple slicing:

```
## One-liner
top_3 = students[np.argsort(sat_scores)][:-4:-1]


## Result
print(top_3)
# ['Alice' 'Frank' 'Carl']
```

Alice, Frank, and Carl have the highest SAT scores of 1543, 1412, and 1343, respectively.

In summary, you've learned about the application of two important NumPy functions: `sort()` and `argsort()`. Next, you'll improve your advanced understanding of NumPy indexing and slicing by using Boolean indexing and lambda functions in a practical data science problem.

How to Use Lambda Functions and Boolean Indexing to Filter Arrays

Real-world data is noisy. As a data scientist, you get paid to get rid of the noise, make the data accessible, and create meaning. Filtering data is therefore vital for real-world data science tasks. In this section, you'll learn how to create a minimal filter function in a single line of code.

The Basics

To create a function in one line, you'll need to use *lambda functions*. As you know from Chapter 2, lambda functions are anonymous functions that you can define in a single line of code:

```
lambda arguments : expression
```

You define a comma-separated list of arguments that serve as inputs. The lambda function then evaluates the expression and returns the result.

Let's explore how to solve our problem by creating a filter function using the lambda function definition.

The Code

Consider the following problem, depicted in Listing 3-24: create a filter function that takes a list of books x and a minimum rating y and returns a list of potential bestsellers that have higher than minimum rating, y'>y.

```
## Dependencies
import numpy as np


## Data (row = [title, rating])
books = np.array([['Coffee Break NumPy', 4.6],
                  ['Lord of the Rings', 5.0],
                  ['Harry Potter', 4.3],
                  ['Winnie-the-Pooh', 3.9],
                  ['The Clown of God', 2.2],
                  ['Coffee Break Python', 4.7]])


## One-liner
predict_bestseller = lambda x, y : x[x[:,1].astype(float) > y]


## Results
print(predict_bestseller(books, 3.9))
```

Listing 3-24: One-liner solution using lambda functions, type conversion, and Boolean operators

Take a guess at the output of this code before moving on.

How It Works

The data consists of a two-dimensional NumPy array in which each row holds the name of the book title and the average user rating (a floating-point number between 0.0 and 5.0). There are six books in the rated data set.

The goal is to create a filter function that takes as input the book rating data set x and a threshold rating y, and returns the books that have a higher rating than the threshold y. You set the threshold to 3.9.

You achieve this by defining an anonymous lambda function that returns the result of the following expression:

```
x[❶x[:,1] ❷.astype(float)❸> y]
```

The array x is assumed to have two columns as our book rating array books. To access the potential bestsellers, you use an advanced indexing scheme similar to the one in Listing 3-17.

First, you carve out the second column ❶ that holds the book ratings and convert it to a float array by using the astype(float) method ❷ on the NumPy array x. This is necessary because the initial array x consists of mixed data types (float and strings).

Second, you create a Boolean array that holds the value True if the book at the respective row index has a rating larger than y ❸. Note that the float y is implicitly broadcasted to a new NumPy array so that both operands of the Boolean operator > have the same shape. At this point, you've created a Boolean array indicating for each book whether it can be considered a bestseller: x[:,1].astype(float)> y = [True True True False False True]. So, the first three books and the last one are bestsellers.

Third, we use the Boolean array as an indexing array on the original book rating array to carve out all the books that have above-threshold ratings. More specifically, we use Boolean indexing x[[True True True False False True]] to get a subarray of the original array with only four books: the ones with True value. This results in the following final output of this one-liner:

```
## Results
print(predict_bestseller(books, 3.9))
"""
[['Coffee Break NumPy' '4.6']
 ['Lord of the Rings' '5.0']
 ['Harry Potter' '4.3']
 ['Coffee Break Python' '4.7']]
"""
```

In summary, you've learned how to filter data using only Boolean indexing and lambda functions. Next, you'll dive into logical operators and learn a useful trick to write the logical and operation concisely.

How to Create Advanced Array Filters with Statistics, Math, and Logic

This section shows you the most basic outlier detection algorithm: if an observed value deviates from the mean by more than the standard deviation, it is considered an *outlier*. You'll work through an example of analyzing website data to determine the number of active users, the bounce rate, and the average session duration in seconds. (The *bounce rate* is the percentage of visitors who leave immediately after visiting only one website. A high bounce rate is a bad signal: it might indicate that a site is boring or irrelevant.) You'll look at the data and identify outliers.

The Basics

To solve the outlier detection problem, you'll first study three basic skills: understanding the mean and standard deviation, finding the absolute value, and performing the logical and operation.

Understanding Mean and Standard Deviation

First, you'll slowly develop our definition of an outlier by using basic statistics. You'll make the basic assumption that all observed data is normally distributed around a mean value. For example, consider the following sequence of data values:

```
[ 8.78087409 10.95890859  8.90183201  8.42516116  9.26643393 12.52747974
  9.70413087 10.09101284  9.90002825 10.15149208  9.42468412 11.36732294
  9.5603904   9.80945055 10.15792838 10.13521324 11.0435137  10.06329581
--snip--
 10.74304416 10.47904781]
```

If you plot the histogram of this sequence, you'll get the result in Figure 3-3.

The sequence seems to resemble a *normal distribution* with a *mean* value of 10 and a *standard deviation* of 1. The mean, denoted with a μ symbol, is the average value of all sequence values. The standard deviation, denoted with a σ symbol, measures the variation of a data set around the mean value. By definition, if the data is truly normally distributed, 68.2 percent of all sample values fall into the standard deviation interval $[\omega_1 = \mu - \sigma, \omega_2 = \mu + \sigma]$. This provides a range for outliers: anything that doesn't fall within the range is considered an outlier.

In the example, I generated the data from the normal distribution $\mu=10$ and $\sigma=1$, which results in the interval $\omega_1 = \mu - 1 = 9$ and $\omega_2 = \mu + 1 = 11$. In the following, you simply assume that *any observed value that is outside the interval marked by the standard deviation around the mean is an outlier*. For our data, this means that any value that doesn't fall into the interval [9,11] is an outlier.

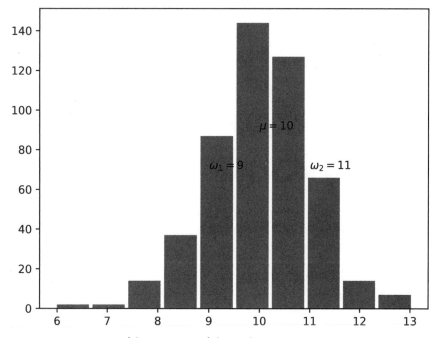

Figure 3-3: Histogram of the sequence of data values

The simple code I used to generate the plot is shown in Listing 3-25. Can you find the code lines that define the mean and standard deviation?

```
import numpy as np
import matplotlib.pyplot as plt

sequence = np.random.normal(10.0, 1.0, 500)
print(sequence)

plt.xkcd()
plt.hist(sequence)
plt.annotate(r"$\omega_1=9$", (9, 70))
plt.annotate(r"$\omega_2=11$", (11, 70))
plt.annotate(r"$\mu=10$", (10, 90))
plt.savefig("plot.jpg")
plt.show()
```

Listing 3-25: Plotting the histogram by using the Matplotlib library

This code shows how to plot a histogram by using Python's Matplotlib library. However, this is not the focus of this section; I want to highlight only how you can create the preceding sequence of data values.

Simply import the NumPy library and use the module np.random, which provides a function normal(mean, deviation, shape) that creates a new NumPy array with values randomly drawn from the normal distribution with a given mean and standard deviation. This is where you set mean=10.0 and deviation=1.0 to create the data in the sequence. In this case, setting shape=500 indicates that you're interested in only a one-dimensional data array with 500 data points. The remaining code imports the special xkcd plot styling plt.xkcd(), plots the histogram based on the sequence using plt.hist(sequence), styles the plot with annotations, and outputs the final plot.

NOTE *The name of the xkcd plot is taken from the popular web comic page xkcd (https://xkcd.com/).*

Before diving into the one-liner, let's quickly explore the other two basic skills you'll need to complete this task.

Finding the Absolute Value

Second, you need to turn negative values into positive, so you can check whether each outlier deviates more than the standard deviation from the mean. You are interested in only the absolute deviation, not in whether it's positive or negative. This is known as taking the *absolute value*. The NumPy function in Listing 3-26 creates a new NumPy array with the absolute values of the original.

```
import numpy as np


a = np.array([1, -1, 2, -2])

print(a)
# [ 1 -1  2 -2]

print(np.abs(a))
# [1 1 2 2]
```

Listing 3-26: Calculating the absolute value in NumPy

The function np.abs() converts the negative values in a NumPy array into their positive counterparts.

Performing the Logical And Operation

Third, the following NumPy function performs an element-wise *logical and* operation to combine two Boolean arrays a and b and give back an array that combines the *individual* Boolean values using the logical and operation (see Listing 3-27).

```
import numpy as np


a = np.array([True, True, True, False])
b = np.array([False, True, True, False])

print(np.logical_and(a, b))
# [False  True  True False]
```

Listing 3-27: The logical and operation applied to NumPy arrays

You combine each element at index *i* of array a with element *i* of array b by using np.logical_and(a, b). The result is an array of Boolean values that are True if both operands a[i] and b[i] are already True, and False otherwise. In this way, you can combine multiple Boolean arrays into a single Boolean array by using standard logical operations. One useful application of this is to combine *Boolean filter arrays* as done in the following one-liner.

Note that you can also *multiply* two Boolean arrays a and b—and this is equivalent to the np.logical_and(a, b) operation. Python represents a True value as an integer value 1 (or really any integer value different from 0) and a False value as an integer value 0. If you multiply anything by 0, you get 0, and therefore False. That means you'll receive a True result (an integer value >1) only when all operands are already True.

With this information, you are now fully equipped to understand the following one-liner code snippet.

The Code

This one-liner will find all outlier days for which the statistics deviate more than the standard deviation from their mean statistics.

```
## Dependencies
import numpy as np


## Website analytics data:
## (row = day), (col = users, bounce, duration)
a = np.array([[815, 70, 115],
              [767, 80, 50],
              [912, 74, 77],
              [554, 88, 70],
              [1008, 65, 128]])
mean, stdev = np.mean(a, axis=0), np.std(a, axis=0)
# [811.2  76.4  88. ], [152.97764543  6.85857128  29.04479299]


## One-liner
outliers = ((np.abs(a[:,0] - mean[0]) > stdev[0])
            * (np.abs(a[:,1] - mean[1]) > stdev[1])
            * (np.abs(a[:,2] - mean[2]) > stdev[2]))


## Result
print(a[outliers])
```

Listing 3-28: One-liner solution using the mean function, standard deviation, and Boolean operators with broadcasting

Can you guess the output of this code snippet?

How It Works

The data set consists of rows that represent different days, and three columns that represent daily active users, bounce rate, and average session duration in seconds, respectively.

For each column, you calculate the mean value and the standard deviation. For example, the mean value of the Daily Active Users column is 811.2, and its standard deviation is 152.97. Note that you use the axis argument in the same way as in "Broadcasting, Slice Assignment, and Reshaping to Clean Every *i*-th Array Element" on page 60.

Our goal is to detect websites that are outliers in all three columns. For the Daily Active Users column, every observed value that is smaller than 811.2 – 152.97 = 658.23 or larger than 811.2 + 152.23 = 963.43 is considered an outlier.

However, you consider a whole *day* to be an outlier only if all three observed columns are outliers. You achieve this by combining the three Boolean arrays using the logical and operator. The result is only a single row for which all three columns are outliers:

```
[[1008   65  128]]
```

In summary, you have learned about the NumPy's logical and operator and how to use it to perform basic outlier detection, while making use of simple statistical measures from the NumPy library. Next, you'll learn about a secret ingredient of Amazon's success: coming up with relevant recommendations of products to buy.

Simple Association Analysis: People Who Bought X Also Bought Y

Have you ever bought a product recommended by Amazon's algorithms? The recommendation algorithms are often based on a technique called *association analysis*. In this section, you'll learn about the basic idea of association analysis and how to dip your toe into the deep ocean of recommender systems.

The Basics

Association analysis is based on historical customer data, such as the "people who bought *x* also bought *y*" data on Amazon. This association of different products is a powerful marketing concept because it not only ties together related but complementary products, but also provides you with an element of *social proof*—knowing that other people have bought a product increases the psychological safety for you to buy the product yourself. This is an excellent tool for marketers.

Let's have a look at a practical example in Figure 3-4.

	📚	🎮	⚽	💻	🎧
Alice	✗	✓	✓	✓	✗
Bob	✓	✗	✓	✗	✓
Louis	✗	✓	✓	?	✗
Larissa	✓	✓	✗	✓	✗

Figure 3-4: Product-Customer matrix—which customer has bought which product?

The four customers Alice, Bob, Louis, and Larissa bought different combinations of the products: book, game, soccer ball, laptop, headphones. Imagine that you know every product bought by all four persons, but not whether Louis has bought the laptop. What do you think: is Louis likely to buy the laptop?

Association analysis (or *collaborative filtering*) provides an answer to this problem. The underlying assumption is that if two people performed similar actions in the past (for example, bought a similar product), they are more likely to keep performing similar actions in the future. Louis has a similar buying behavior to Alice, and Alice bought the laptop. Thus, the recommender system predicts that Louis is likely to buy the laptop too.

The following code snippet simplifies this problem.

The Code

Consider the following problem: what fraction of customers bought two ebooks together? Based on this data, the recommender system can offer customers a book "bundle" to buy if it sees that they originally intended to buy a single book. See Listing 3-29.

```
## Dependencies
import numpy as np


## Data: row is customer shopping basket
## row = [course 1, course 2, ebook 1, ebook 2]
## value 1 indicates that an item was bought.
basket = np.array([[0, 1, 1, 0],
                   [0, 0, 0, 1],
                   [1, 1, 0, 0],
                   [0, 1, 1, 1],
                   [1, 1, 1, 0],
                   [0, 1, 1, 0],
                   [1, 1, 0, 1],
                   [1, 1, 1, 1]])
```

```
## One-liner
copurchases = np.sum(np.all(basket[:,2:], axis = 1)) / basket.shape[0]


## Result
print(copurchases)
```

Listing 3-29: One-liner solution using slicing, the axis argument, the shape property, and basic array arithmetic with broadcasting

What is the output of this code snippet?

How It Works

The basket data array contains one row per customer and one column per product. The first two products with column indices 0 and 1 are online courses, and the latter two with column indices 2 and 3 are ebooks. The value 1 in cell (i,j) indicates that customer i has bought the product j.

Our task is to find the fraction of customers who bought both ebooks, so we're interested in only columns 2 and 3. First, then, you carve out the relevant columns from the original array to get the following subarray:

```
print(basket[:,2:])
"""
[[1 0]
 [0 1]
 [0 0]
 [1 1]
 [1 0]
 [1 0]
 [0 1]
 [1 1]]
"""
```

This gives you an array of only the third and the fourth columns.

The NumPy all() function checks whether all values in a NumPy array evaluate to True. If this is the case, it returns True. Otherwise, it returns False. When used with the axis argument, the function performs this operation along the specified axis.

You'll notice that the axis argument is a recurring element for many NumPy functions, so it's worth taking your time to understand the axis argument properly. The specified axis is collapsed into a single value based on the respective aggregator function (all() in this case).

Thus, the result of applying the all() function on the subarray is the following:

```
print(np.all(basket[:,2:], axis = 1))
# [False False False  True False False False  True]
```

In plain English: only the fourth and the last customers have bought both ebooks.

Because you are interested in the fraction of customers, you sum over this Boolean array, giving you a total of 2, and divide by the number of customers, 8. The result is 0.25, the fraction of customers who bought both ebooks.

In summary, you've strengthened your understanding of NumPy fundamentals such as the shape attribute and the axis argument, as well as how to combine them to analyze copurchases of different products. Next, you'll stay with this example and learn about more advanced array aggregation techniques using a combination of NumPy's and Python's special capabilities—that is, *broadcasting* and *list comprehension*.

Intermediate Association Analysis to Find Bestseller Bundles

Let's explore the topic of association analysis in more detail.

The Basics

Consider the example of the previous section: your customers purchase individual products from a corpus of four different products. Your company wants to upsell related products (offer a customer an additional, often related, product to buy). For each combination of products, you need to calculate how often they've been purchased by the same customer, and find the two products purchased together most often.

For this problem, you've already learned everything you need to know, so let's dive right in!

The Code

This one-liner aims to find the two items that were purchased most often together; see Listing 3-30.

```
## Dependencies
import numpy as np


## Data: row is customer shopping basket
## row = [course 1, course 2, ebook 1, ebook 2]
## value 1 indicates that an item was bought.
basket = np.array([[0, 1, 1, 0],
                   [0, 0, 0, 1],
                   [1, 1, 0, 0],
                   [0, 1, 1, 1],
                   [1, 1, 1, 0],
                   [0, 1, 1, 0],
                   [1, 1, 0, 1],
                   [1, 1, 1, 1]])


## One-liner (broken down in two lines;)
copurchases = [(i,j,np.sum(basket[:,i] + basket[:,j] == 2))
```

```
          for i in range(4) for j in range(i+1,4)]

## Result
print(max(copurchases, key=lambda x:x[2]))
```

Listing 3-30: One-liner solution using a lambda function as the max() function's key parameter, list comprehension, and Boolean operators with broadcasting

What's the output of this one-liner solution?

How It Works

The data array consists of historical purchasing data with one row per customer and one column per product. Our goal is to get a list of tuples: each tuple describes a combination of products and how often that combination was bought together. For each list element, you want the first two tuple values to be column indices (the combination of two products) and the third tuple value to be the number of times these products were bought together. For example, the tuple (0,1,4) indicates that customers who bought *product 0* also bought *product 1* four times.

So how can you achieve this? Let's break down the one-liner, reformatted a little here as it's too wide to fit on a single line:

```
## One-liner (broken down in two lines;)
copurchases = [(i,j,np.sum(basket[:,i] + basket[:,j] == 2))
               for i in range(4) for j in range(i+1,4)]
```

You can see in the outer format [(..., ..., ...) for ... in ... for ... in ...] that you create a list of tuples by using list comprehension (see Chapter 2). You're interested in every unique combination of column indices of an array with four columns. Here's the result of just the outer part of this one-liner:

```
print([(i,j) for i in range(4) for j in range(i+1,4)])
# [(0, 1), (0, 2), (0, 3), (1, 2), (1, 3), (2, 3)]
```

So, there are six tuples in the list, each a unique combination of column indices.

Knowing this, you can now dive into the third tuple element: the number of times these two products i and j have been bought together:

```
np.sum(basket[:,i] + basket[:,j] == 2)
```

You use slicing to extract both columns i and j from the original NumPy array. Then you add them together element-wise. For the resulting array, you check element-wise whether the sum is equal to 2, which would indicate that there was a 1 in both columns and so both products have been purchased together. The result is a Boolean array with True values if two products have been purchased together by a single customer.

You store all resulting tuples in the list copurchases. Here are the elements of the list:

```
print(copurchases)
# [(0, 1, 4), (0, 2, 2), (0, 3, 2), (1, 2, 5), (1, 3, 3), (2, 3, 2)]
```

Now there is one thing left: find the two products that have been co-purchased most often:

```
## Result
print(max(copurchases, key=lambda x:x[2]))
```

You use the max() function to find the maximum element in the list. You define a key function that takes a tuple and returns the third tuple value (number of copurchases), and then find the max out of those values. The result of the one-liner is as follows:

```
## Result
print(max(copurchases, key=lambda x:x[2]))
# (1, 2, 5)
```

The second and third products have been purchased together five times. No other product combination reaches copurchasing power this high. Hence, you can tell your boss to upsell *product 2* when selling *product 1*, and vice versa.

In summary, you've learned about various core features of both Python and NumPy, such as broadcasting, list comprehension, lambda functions, and the key function. Often, the expressive power of your Python code emerges from the combination of multiple language elements, functions, and code tricks.

Summary

In this chapter, you learned elementary NumPy basics such as array, shape, axis, type, broadcasting, advanced indexing, slicing, sorting, searching, aggregating, and statistics. You've also improved your basic Python skills by practicing important techniques such as list comprehension, logics, and lambda functions. Last but not least, you've improved your ability to read, understand, and write concise code quickly, while mastering fundamental data science problems on the way.

Let's keep this fast pace of studying various interesting topics in the Python space. Next, you'll dive into the exciting topic of machine learning. You'll learn about basic machine learning algorithms and how to leverage their powerful capabilities in a single line of code by using the popular scikit-learn library. Every machine learning expert knows this library very well. But fear not—your freshly acquired NumPy skills will help you greatly in understanding the code snippets covered next.

4

MACHINE LEARNING

Machine learning is found in almost every area of computer science. Over the past few years, I've attended computer science conferences in fields as diverse as distributed systems, databases, and stream processing, and no matter where I go, machine learning is already there. At some conferences, more than half of the presented research ideas have relied on machine learning methods.

As a computer scientist, you must know the fundamental machine learning ideas and algorithms to round out your overall skill set. This chapter provides an introduction to the most important machine learning algorithms and methods, and gives you 10 practical one-liners to apply these algorithms in your own projects.

The Basics of Supervised Machine Learning

The main aim of machine learning is to make accurate predictions using existing data. Let's say you want to write an algorithm that predicts the value of a specific stock over the next two days. To achieve this goal, you'll need to train a machine learning model. But what exactly is a *model*?

From the perspective of a machine learning user, the machine learning model looks like a black box (Figure 4-1): you put data in and get predictions out.

Figure 4-1: A machine learning model, shown as a black box

In this model, you call the input data *features* and denote them using the variable *x*, which can be a numerical value or a multidimensional vector of numerical values. Then the box does its magic and processes your input data. After a bit of time, you get prediction *y* back, which is the model's predicted output, given the input features. For regression problems, the prediction consists of one or multiple numerical values—just like the input features.

Supervised machine learning is divided into two separate phases: the training phase and the inference phase.

Training Phase

During the *training phase*, you tell your model your desired output y' for a given input *x*. When the model outputs the prediction *y*, you compare it to y', and if they are not the same, you update the model to generate an output that is closer to y', as shown in Figure 4-2. Let's look at an example from image recognition. Say you train a model to predict fruit names (outputs) when given images (inputs). For example, your specific training input is an image of a banana, but your model wrongly predicts *apple*. Because your desired output is different from the model prediction, you change the model so that next time the model will correctly predict *banana*.

Figure 4-2: The training phase of a machine learning model

As you keep telling the model your desired outputs for many different inputs and adjusting the model, you train the model by using your *training data*. Over time, the model will learn which output you'd like to get for certain inputs. That's why data is so important in the 21st century: your model will be only as good as its training data. Without good training data, the model is guaranteed to fail. Roughly speaking, the training data supervises the machine learning process. That's why we denote it *supervised learning*.

Inference Phase

During the *inference phase*, you use the trained model to predict output values for new input features x. Note that the model has the power to predict outputs for inputs that have never been observed in the training data. For example, the fruit prediction model from the *training phase* can now identify the name of the fruits (learned in the training data) in images it has never seen before. In other words, suitable machine learning models possess the ability to *generalize*: they use their experience from the training data to predict outcomes for new inputs. Roughly speaking, models that generalize well produce accurate predictions for new input data. Generalized prediction for unseen input data is one of the strengths of machine learning and is a prime reason for its popularity across a wide range of applications.

Linear Regression

Linear regression is the one machine learning algorithm you'll find most often in beginner-level machine learning tutorials. It's commonly used in *regression problems*, for which the model predicts missing data values by using existing ones. A considerable advantage of linear regression, both for teachers and users, is its simplicity. But that doesn't mean it can't solve real problems! Linear regression has lots of practical use cases in diverse areas such as market research, astronomy, and biology. In this section, you'll learn everything you need to know to get started with linear regression.

The Basics

How can you use linear regression to predict stock prices on a given day? Before I answer this question, let's start with some definitions.

Every machine learning model consists of model parameters. *Model parameters* are internal configuration variables that are estimated from the data. These model parameters determine how exactly the model calculates the prediction, given the input features. For linear regression, the model parameters are called *coefficients*. You may remember the formula for two-dimensional lines from school: $f(x) = ax + c$. The two variables a and c are the coefficients in the linear equation $ax + c$. You can describe how each input x is transformed into an output $f(x)$ so that all outputs together describe a line in the two-dimensional space. By changing the coefficients, you can describe any line in the two-dimensional space.

Given the input features x_1, x_2, . . ., x_k, the linear regression model combines the input features with the coefficients a_1, a_2, . . ., a_k to calculate the predicted output y by using this formula:

$$y = f(x) = a_0 + a_1 \times x_1 + a_2 \times x_2 + \ldots + a_k \times x_k$$

In our stock price example, you have a single input feature, x, the day. You input the day x with the hope of getting a stock price, the output y. This simplifies the linear regression model to the formula of a two-dimensional line:

$$y = f(x) = a_0 + a_1 x$$

Let's have a look at three lines for which you change only the two model parameters a_0 and a_1 in Figure 4-3. The first axis describes the input x. The second axis describes the output y. The line represents the (linear) relationship between input and output.

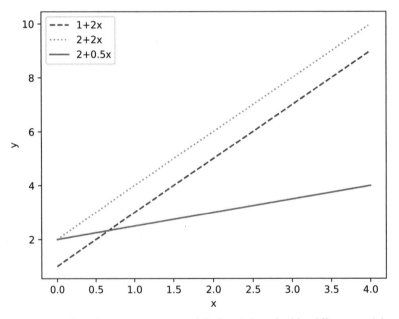

Figure 4-3: Three linear regression models (lines) described by different model parameters (coefficients). Every line represents a unique relationship between the input and the output variables.

In our stock price example, let's say our training data is the indices of three days, [0, 1, 2], matched with the stock prices [155, 156, 157]. To put it differently:

- Input x=0 should cause output y=155
- Input x=1 should cause output y=156
- Input x=2 should cause output y=157

Now, which line best fits our training data? I plotted the training data in Figure 4-4.

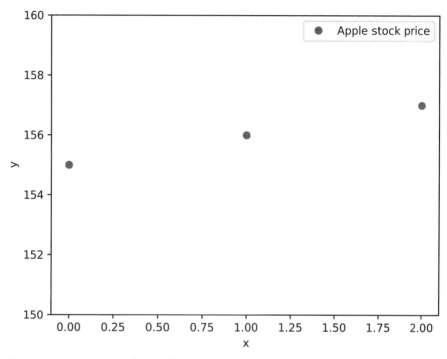

Figure 4-4: Our training data, with its index in the array as the x coordinate, and its price as the y coordinate

To find the line that best describes the data and, thus, to create a linear regression model, we need to determine the coefficients. This is where machine learning comes in. There are two principal ways of determining model parameters for linear regression. First, you can analytically calculate the line of best fit that goes between these points (the standard method for linear regression). Second, you can try different models, testing each against the labeled sample data, and ultimately deciding on the best one. In any case, you determine "best" through a process called *error minimization*, in which the model minimizes the squared difference (or selects the coefficients that lead to a minimal squared difference) of the predicted model values and the ideal output, selecting the model with the lowest error.

For our data, you end up with coefficients of $a_0 = 155.0$ and $a_1 = 1.0$. Then you put them into our formula for linear regression:

$$y = f(x) = a_0 + a_1 x = 155.0 + 1.0 \times x$$

and plot both the line and the training data in the same space, as shown in Figure 4-5.

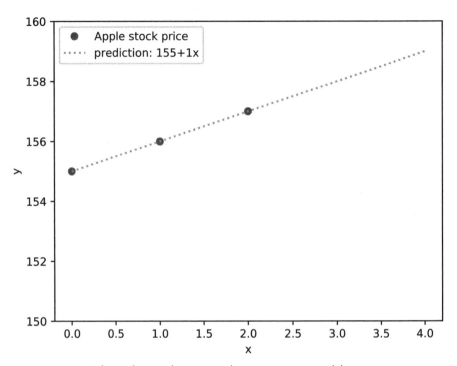

Figure 4-5: A prediction line made using our linear regression model

A perfect fit! The squared distance between the line (model prediction) and the training data is zero—so you have found the model that minimizes the error. Using this model, you can now predict the stock price for any value of x. For example, say you want to predict the stock price on day $x = 4$. To accomplish this, you simply use the model to calculate $f(x) = 155.0 + 1.0 \times 4 = 159.0$. The predicted stock price on day 4 is \$159. Of course, whether this prediction accurately reflects the real world is another story.

That's the high-level overview of what happens. Let's take a closer look at how to do this in code.

The Code

Listing 4-1 shows how to build a simple linear regression model in a single line of code (you may need to install the scikit-learn library first by running `pip install sklearn` in your shell).

```
from sklearn.linear_model import LinearRegression
import numpy as np

## Data (Apple stock prices)
apple = np.array([155, 156, 157])
n = len(apple)
```

```
## One-liner
model = LinearRegression().fit(np.arange(n).reshape((n,1)), apple)

## Result & puzzle
print(model.predict([[3],[4]]))
```

Listing 4-1: A simple linear regression model

Can you already guess the output of this code snippet?

How It Works

This one-liner uses two Python libraries: NumPy and scikit-learn. The former is the de facto standard library for numerical computations (like matrix operations). The latter is the most comprehensive library for machine learning and has implementations of hundreds of machine learning algorithms and techniques.

You may ask: "Why are you using libraries in a Python one-liner? Isn't this cheating?" It's a good question, and the answer is yes. Any Python program—with or without libraries—uses high-level functionality built on low-level operations. There's not much point in reinventing the wheel when you can reuse existing code bases (that is, stand on the shoulders of giants). Aspiring coders often feel the urge to implement everything on their own, but this reduces their coding productivity. In this book, we're going to use, not reject, the wide spectrum of powerful functionality implemented by some of the world's best Python coders and pioneers. Each of these libraries took skilled coders years to develop, optimize, and tweak.

Let's go through Listing 4-1 step by step. First, we create a simple data set of three values and store its length in a separate variable n to make the code more concise. Our data is three Apple stock prices for three consecutive days. The variable apple holds this data set as a one-dimensional NumPy array.

Second, we build the model by calling LinearRegression(). But what are the model parameters? To find them, we call the fit() function to train the model. The fit() function takes two arguments: the input features of the training data and the ideal outputs for these inputs. Our ideal outputs are the real stock prices of the Apple stock. But for the input features, fit() requires an array with the following format:

```
[<training_data_1>,
<training_data_2>,
--snip--
<training_data_n>]
```

where each training data value is a sequence of feature values:

```
<training_data> = [feature_1, feature_2, ..., feature_k]
```

In our case, the input consists of only a single feature *x* (the current day). Moreover, the prediction also consists of only a single value *y* (the current stock price). To bring the input array into the correct shape, you need to reshape it to this strange-looking matrix form:

```
[[0],
 [1],
 [2]]
```

A matrix with only one column is called a *column vector*. You use np.arange() to create the sequence of increasing *x* values; then you use reshape((n, 1)) to convert the one-dimensional NumPy array into a two-dimensional array with one column and n rows (see Chapter 3). Note that scikit-learn allows the output to be a one-dimensional array (otherwise, you would have to reshape the apple data array as well).

Once it has the training data and the ideal outputs, fit() then does error minimization: it finds the model parameters (that means *line*) so that the difference between the predicted model values and the desired outputs is minimal.

When fit() is satisfied with its model, it'll return a model that you can use to predict two new stock values by using the predict() function. The predict() function has the same input requirements as fit(), so to satisfy them, you'll pass a one-column matrix with our two new values that you want predictions for:

```
print(model.predict([[3],[4]]))
```

Because our error minimization was zero, you should get perfectly linear outputs of 158 and 159. This fits well along the line of fit plotted in Figure 4-5. But it's often not possible to find such a perfectly fitting single straight-line linear model. For example, if our stock prices are [157, 156, 159], and you run the same function and plot it, you should get the line in Figure 4-6.

In this case, the fit() function finds the line that minimizes the squared error between the training data and the predictions as described previously.

Let's wrap this up. Linear regression is a machine learning technique whereby your model learns coefficients as model parameters. The resulting linear model (for example, a line in the two-dimensional space) directly provides you with predictions on new input data. This problem of predicting numerical values when given numerical input values belongs to the class of regression problems. In the next section, you'll learn about another important area in machine learning called classification.

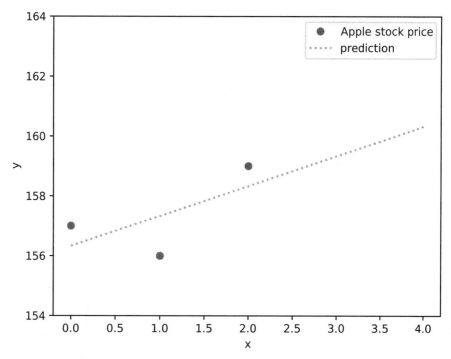

Figure 4-6: A linear regression model with an imperfect fit

Logistic Regression in One Line

Logistic regression is commonly used for *classification problems*, in which you predict whether a sample belongs to a specific category (or class). This contrasts with regression problems, where you're given a sample and predict a numerical value that falls into a continuous range. An example classification problem is to divide Twitter users into the male and female, given different input features such as their *posting frequency* or the *number of tweet replies*. The logistic regression model belongs to one of the most fundamental machine learning models. Many concepts introduced in this section will be the basis of more advanced machine learning techniques.

The Basics

To introduce logistic regression, let's briefly review how linear regression works: given the training data, you compute a line that fits this training data and predicts the outcome for input *x*. In general, linear regression is great for predicting a *continuous* output, whose value can take an infinite number of values. The stock price predicted earlier, for example, could conceivably have been any number of positive values.

But what if the output is not continuous, but *categorical*, belonging to a limited number of groups or categories? For example, let's say you want to predict the likelihood of lung cancer, given the number of cigarettes a patient smokes. Each patient can either have lung cancer or not. In contrast to the stock price, here you have only these two possible outcomes. Predicting the likelihood of categorical outcomes is the primary motivation for logistic regression.

The Sigmoid Function

Whereas linear regression fits a line to the training data, logistic regression fits an S-shaped curve, called *the sigmoid function*. The S-shaped curve helps you make binary decisions (for example, yes/no). For most input values, the sigmoid function will return a value that is either very close to 0 (one category) or very close to 1 (the other category). It's relatively unlikely that your given input value generates an ambiguous output. Note that it is possible to generate 0.5 probabilities for a given input value—but the shape of the curve is designed in a way to minimize those in practical settings (for most possible values on the horizontal axis, the probability value is either very close to 0 or very close to 1). Figure 4-7 shows a logistic regression curve for the lung cancer scenario.

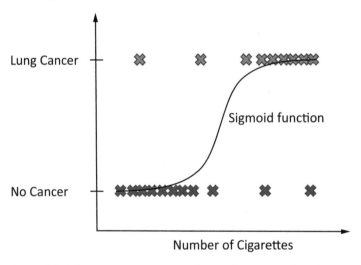

Figure 4-7: A logistic regression curve that predicts cancer based on cigarette use

NOTE *You can apply logistic regression for* multinomial classification *to classify the data into more than two classes. To accomplish this, you'll use the generalization of the sigmoid function, called the* softmax function, *which returns a tuple of probabilities, one for each class. The sigmoid function transforms the input feature(s) into only a single probability value. However, for clarity and readability, I'll focus on* binomial classification *and the sigmoid function in this section.*

The sigmoid function in Figure 4-7 approximates the probability that a patient has lung cancer, given the number of cigarettes they smoke. This probability helps you make a robust decision on the subject when the only information you have is the number of cigarettes the patient smokes: does the patient have lung cancer?

Have a look at the predictions in Figure 4-8, which shows two new patients (in light gray at the bottom of the graph). You know nothing about them but the number of cigarettes they smoke. You've trained our logistic regression model (the sigmoid function) that returns a probability value for any new input value x. If the probability given by the sigmoid function is higher than 50 percent, the model predicts *lung cancer positive*; otherwise, it predicts *lung cancer negative*.

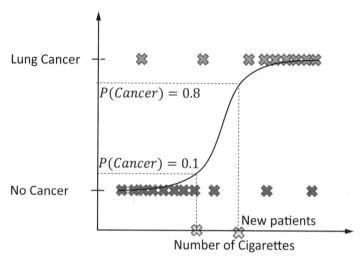

Figure 4-8: Using logistic regression to estimate probabilities of a result

Finding the Maximum Likelihood Model

The main question for logistic regression is how to select the correct sigmoid function that best fits the training data. The answer is in each model's *likelihood:* the probability that the model would generate the observed training data. You want to select the model with the maximum likelihood. Your sense is that this model best approximates the real-world process that generated the training data.

To calculate the likelihood of a given model for a given set of training data, you calculate the likelihood for each single training data point, and then multiply those with each other to get the likelihood of the whole set of training data. How to calculate the likelihood of a single training data point? Simply apply this model's sigmoid function to the training data point; it'll give you the data point's probability under this model. To select the maximum likelihood model for all data points, you repeat this same likelihood computation for different sigmoid functions (shifting the sigmoid function a little bit), as in Figure 4-9.

In the previous paragraph, I described how to determine the maximum likelihood sigmoid function (model). This sigmoid function fits the data best—so you can use it to predict new data points.

Now that we've covered the theory, let's look at how you'd implement logistic regression as a Python one-liner.

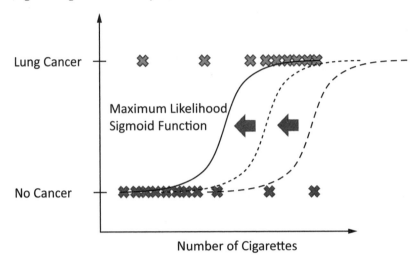

Figure 4-9: Testing several sigmoid functions to determine maximum likelihood

The Code

You've seen an example of using logistic regression for a health application (correlating cigarette consumption with cancer probability). This "virtual doc" application would be a great idea for a smartphone app, wouldn't it? Let's program your first virtual doc using logistic regression, as shown in Listing 4-2—in a single line of Python code!

```
from sklearn.linear_model import LogisticRegression
import numpy as np


## Data (#cigarettes, cancer)
X = np.array([[0, "No"],
              [10, "No"],
              [60, "Yes"],
              [90, "Yes"]])


## One-liner
model = LogisticRegression().fit(X[:,0].reshape(n,1), X[:,1])


## Result & puzzle
print(model.predict([[2],[12],[13],[40],[90]]))
```

Listing 4-2: A logistic regression model

Take a guess: what's the output of this code snippet?

How It Works

The training data X consists of four patient records (the rows) with two columns. The first column holds the number of cigarettes the patients smoke (*input feature*), and the second column holds the *class labels*, which say whether they ultimately suffered from lung cancer.

You create the model by calling the LogisticRegression() constructor. You call the fit() function on this model; fit() takes two arguments, which are the input (cigarette consumption) and the output class labels (cancer). The fit() function expects a two-dimensional input array format with one row per training data sample and one column per feature of this training data sample. In this case, you have only a single feature value so you transform the one-dimensional input into a two-dimensional NumPy array by using the reshape() operation. The first argument to reshape() specifies the number of rows, and the second specifies the number of columns. You care about only the number of columns, which here is 1. You'll pass -1 as the number of desired rows, which is a special signal to NumPy to determine the number of rows automatically.

The input training data will look as follows after reshaping (in essence, you simply remove the class labels and keep the two-dimensional array shape intact):

```
[[0],
 [10],
 [60],
 [90]]
```

Next, you predict whether a patient has lung cancer, given the number of cigarettes they smoke: your input will be 2, 12, 13, 40, 90 cigarettes. That gives an output as follows:

```
# ['No' 'No' 'Yes' 'Yes' 'Yes']
```

The model predicts that the first two patients are lung cancer negative, while the latter three are lung cancer positive.

Let's look in detail at the probabilities the sigmoid function came up with that lead to this prediction! Simply run the following code snippet after Listing 4-2:

```
for i in range(20):
    print("x=" + str(i) + " --> " + str(model.predict_proba([[i]])))
```

The predict_proba() function takes as input the number of cigarettes and returns an array containing the probability of lung cancer negative (at index 0) and the probability of lung cancer positive (index 1). When you run this code, you should get the following output:

```
x=0 --> [[0.67240789 0.32759211]]
x=1 --> [[0.65961501 0.34038499]]
x=2 --> [[0.64658514 0.35341486]]
```

```
x=3  --> [[0.63333374 0.36666626]]
x=4  --> [[0.61987758 0.38012242]]
x=5  --> [[0.60623463 0.39376537]]
x=6  --> [[0.59242397 0.40757603]]
x=7  --> [[0.57846573 0.42153427]]
x=8  --> [[0.56438097 0.43561903]]
x=9  --> [[0.55019154 0.44980846]]
x=10 --> [[0.53591997 0.46408003]]
x=11 --> [[0.52158933 0.47841067]]
x=12 --> [[0.50722306 0.49277694]]
x=13 --> [[0.49284485 0.50715515]]
x=14 --> [[0.47847846 0.52152154]]
x=15 --> [[0.46414759 0.53585241]]
x=16 --> [[0.44987569 0.55012431]]
x=17 --> [[0.43568582 0.56431418]]
x=18 --> [[0.42160051 0.57839949]]
x=19 --> [[0.40764163 0.59235837]]
```

If the probability of lung cancer being negative is higher than the probability of lung cancer being positive, the predicted outcome will be *lung cancer negative*. This happens the last time for x=12. If the patient has smoked more than 12 cigarettes, the algorithm will classify them as *lung cancer positive*.

In summary, you've learned how to classify problems easily with logistic regression using the scikit-learn library. The idea of logistic regression is to fit an S-shaped curve (the sigmoid function) to the data. This function assigns a numerical value between 0 and 1 to every new data point and each possible class. The numerical value models the probability of this data point belonging to the given class. However, in practice, you often have training data but no class label assigned to the training data. For example, you have customer data (say, their age and their income) but you don't know any class label for each data point. To still extract useful insights from this kind of data, you will learn about another category of machine learning next: unsupervised learning. Specifically, you'll learn about how to find similar clusters of data points, an important subset of unsupervised learning.

K-Means Clustering in One Line

If there's one clustering algorithm you need to know—whether you're a computer scientist, data scientist, or machine learning expert—it's the *K-Means algorithm*. In this section, you'll learn the general idea and when and how to use it in a single line of Python code.

The Basics

The previous sections covered supervised learning, in which the training data is *labeled*. In other words, you know the output value of every input value in the training data. But in practice, this isn't always the case. Often, you'll find yourself confronted with *unlabeled* data—especially in many data analytics applications—where it's not clear what "the optimal output" means. In these situations, a prediction is impossible (because there is no output to start with), but you can still distill useful knowledge from these unlabeled data sets (for example, you can find clusters of similar unlabeled data). Models that use unlabeled data fall under the category of *unsupervised learning*.

As an example, suppose you're working in a startup that serves different target markets with various income levels and ages. Your boss tells you to find a certain number of target personas that best fit your target markets. You can use clustering methods to identify the *average customer personas* that your company serves. Figure 4-10 shows an example.

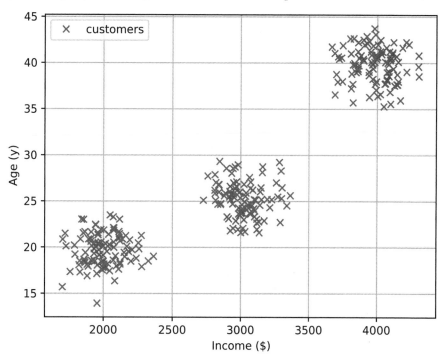

Figure 4-10: Observed customer data in the two-dimensional space

Here, you can easily identify three types of personas with different types of incomes and ages. But how to find those algorithmically? This is the domain of clustering algorithms such as the widely popular K-Means algorithm. Given the data sets and an integer k, the K-Means algorithm finds k clusters of data such that the difference between the center of a cluster (called the *centroid*) and the data in the cluster is minimal. In other words, you can find the different personas by running the K-Means algorithm on your data sets, as shown in Figure 4-11.

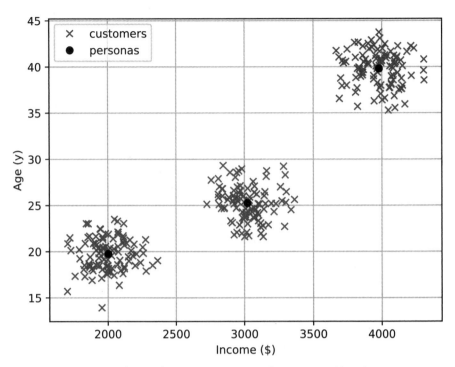

Figure 4-11: Customer data with customer personas (cluster centroids) in the two-dimensional space

The cluster centers (black dots) match the clustered customer data. Every cluster center can be viewed as one customer persona. Thus, you have three idealized personas: a 20-year-old earning $2000, a 25-year-old earning $3000, and a 40-year-old earning $4000. And the great thing is that the K-Means algorithm finds those cluster centers even in high-dimensional spaces (where it would be hard for humans to find the personas visually).

The K-Means algorithm requires "the number of cluster centers k" as an input. In this case, you look at the data and "magically" define $k = 3$. More advanced algorithms can find the number of cluster centers automatically (for an example, look at the 2004 paper "Learning the k in K-Means" by Greg Hamerly and Charles Elkan).

So how does the K-Means algorithm work? In a nutshell, it performs the following procedure:

```
Initialize random cluster centers (centroids).
Repeat until convergence
    Assign every data point to its closest cluster center.
Recompute each cluster center as the centroid of all data points assigned to it.
```

This results in multiple loop iterations: you first assign the data to the *k* cluster centers, and then you recompute each cluster center as the centroid of the data assigned to it.

Let's implement it!

Consider the following problem: given two-dimensional salary data (*hours worked, salary earned*), find two clusters of employees in the given data set that work a similar number of hours and earn a similar salary.

The Code

How can you do all of this in a single line of code? Fortunately, the scikit-learn library in Python already has an efficient implementation of the K-Means algorithm. Listing 4-3 shows the one-liner code snippet that runs K-Means clustering for you.

```
## Dependencies
from sklearn.cluster import KMeans
import numpy as np


## Data (Work (h) / Salary ($))
X = np.array([[35, 7000], [45, 6900], [70, 7100],
              [20, 2000], [25, 2200], [15, 1800]])


## One-liner
kmeans = KMeans(n_clusters=2).fit(X)


## Result & puzzle
cc = kmeans.cluster_centers_
print(cc)
```

Listing 4-3: K-Means clustering in one line

What's the output of this code snippet? Try to guess a solution even if you don't understand every syntactical detail. This will open your knowledge gap and prepare your brain to absorb the algorithm much better.

How It Works

In the first lines, you import the KMeans module from the sklearn.cluster package. This module takes care of the clustering itself. You also need to import the NumPy library because the KMeans module works on NumPy arrays.

Our data is two-dimensional. It correlates the number of working hours with the salary of some workers. Figure 4-12 shows the six data points in this employee data set.

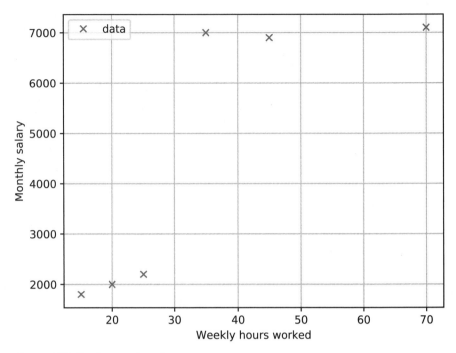

Figure 4-12: Employee salary data

The goal is to find the two cluster centers that best fit this data:

```
## One-liner
kmeans = KMeans(n_clusters=2).fit(X)
```

In the one-liner, you create a new KMeans object that handles the algorithm for you. When you create the KMeans object, you define the number of cluster centers by using the n_clusters function argument. Then you simply call the instance method fit(X) to run the K-Means algorithm on the input data X. The KMeans object now holds all the results. All that's left is to retrieve the results from its attributes:

```
cc = kmeans.cluster_centers_
print(cc)
```

Note that in the sklearn package, the convention is to use a trailing underscore for some attribute names (for example, cluster_centers_) to indicate that these attributes were created dynamically within the training phase (the fit() function). Before the training phase, these attributes do not exist yet. This is not general Python convention (trailing underscores are usually used only to avoid naming conflicts with Python keywords—variable list_ instead of list). However, if you get used to it, you appreciate the consistent use of attributes in the sklearn package. So, what are the cluster centers and what is the output of this code snippet? Take a look at Figure 4-13.

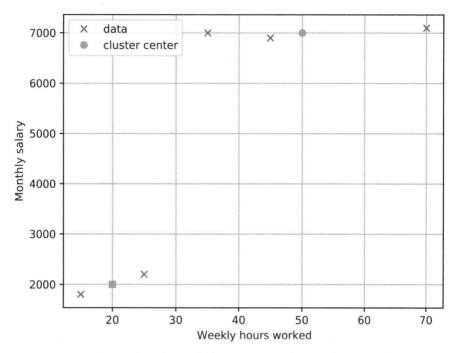

Figure 4-13: Employee salary data with cluster centers in the two-dimensional space

You can see that the two cluster centers are (20, 2000) and (50, 7000). This is also the result of the Python one-liner. These clusters correspond to two idealized employee personas: the first works for 20 hours a week and earns $2000 per month, while the second works for 50 hours a week and earns $7000 per month. Those two types of personas fit the data reasonably well. Thus, the result of the one-liner code snippet is as follows:

```
## Result & puzzle
cc = kmeans.cluster_centers_
print(cc)
'''
[[  50. 7000.]
 [  20. 2000.]]
'''
```

To summarize, this section introduced you to an important subtopic of unsupervised learning: clustering. The K-Means algorithm is a simple, efficient, and popular way of extracting k clusters from multidimensional data. Behind the scenes, the algorithm iteratively recomputes cluster centers and reassigns each data value to its closest cluster center until it finds the optimal clusters. But clusters are not always ideal for finding similar data items. Many data sets do not show a clustered behavior, but you'll still want to leverage the distance information for machine learning and prediction. Let's stay in the multidimensional space and explore another way to use the distance of (Euclidean) data values: the K-Nearest Neighbors algorithm.

K-Nearest Neighbors in One Line

The popular *K-Nearest Neighbors (KNN)* algorithm is used for regression and classification in many applications such as recommender systems, image classification, and financial data forecasting. It's the basis of many advanced machine learning techniques (for example, in information retrieval). There is no doubt that understanding KNN is an important building block of your proficient computer science education.

The Basics

The KNN algorithm is a robust, straightforward, and popular machine learning method. It's simple to implement but still a competitive and fast machine learning technique. All other machine learning models we've discussed so far use the training data to compute a *representation* of the original data. You can use this representation to predict, classify, or cluster new data. For example, the linear and logistic regression algorithms define learning parameters, while the clustering algorithm calculates cluster centers based on the training data. However, the KNN algorithm is different. In contrast to the other approaches, it does not compute a new model (or representation) but uses the *whole data set* as a model.

Yes, you read that right. The machine learning model is nothing more than a set of observations. Every single instance of your training data is one part of your model. This has advantages and disadvantages. A disadvantage is that the model can quickly blow up as the training data grows—which may require sampling or filtering as a preprocessing step. A great advantage, however, is the simplicity of the training phase (just add the new data values to the model). Additionally, you can use the KNN algorithm for prediction or classification. You execute the following strategy, given your input vector x:

1. Find the k nearest neighbors of x (according to a predefined distance metric).

2. Aggregate the k nearest neighbors into a single prediction or classification value. You can use any aggregator function such as average, mean, max, or min.

Let's walk through an example. Your company sells homes for clients. It has acquired a large database of customers and house prices (see Figure 4-14). One day, your client asks how much they must expect to pay for a house of 52 square meters. You query your KNN model, and it immediately gives you the response $33,167. And indeed, your client finds a home for $33,489 the same week. How did the KNN system come to this surprisingly accurate prediction?

First, the KNN system simply calculates the $k = 3$ nearest neighbors to the query $D = 52$ *square meters* using Euclidean distance. The three nearest neighbors are A, B, and C with prices $34,000, $33,500, and $32,000, respectively. Then, it aggregates the three nearest neighbors by calculating the simple average of their values. Because $k = 3$ in this example, you denote the model as *3NN*. Of course, you can vary the similarity functions, the parameter *k*, and the aggregation method to come up with more sophisticated prediction models.

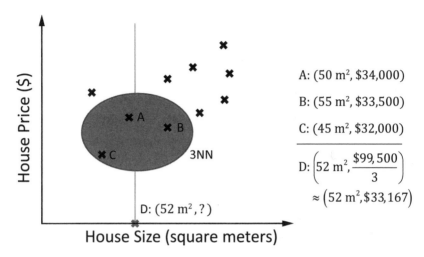

Figure 4-14: Calculating the price of house D based on the three nearest neighbors A, B, and C

Another advantage of KNN is that it can be easily adapted as new observations are made. This is not generally true for machine learning models. An obvious weakness in this regard is that as the computational complexity of finding the *k* nearest neighbors becomes harder and harder, the more points you add. To accommodate for that, you can continuously remove stale values from the model.

As I mentioned, you can also use KNN for classification problems. Instead of averaging over the *k* nearest neighbors, you can use a voting mechanism: each nearest neighbor votes for its class, and the class with the most votes wins.

The Code

Let's dive into how to use KNN in Python—in a single line of code (see Listing 4-4).

```
## Dependencies
from sklearn.neighbors import KNeighborsRegressor
import numpy as np


## Data (House Size (square meters) / House Price ($))
X = np.array([[35, 30000], [45, 45000], [40, 50000],
              [35, 35000], [25, 32500], [40, 40000]])


## One-liner
KNN = KNeighborsRegressor(n_neighbors=3).fit(X[:,0].reshape(-1,1), X[:,1])
```

```
## Result & puzzle
res = KNN.predict([[30]])
print(res)
```

Listing 4-4: Running the KNN algorithm in one line of Python

Take a guess: what's the output of this code snippet?

How It Works

To help you see the result, let's plot the housing data from this code in Figure 4-15.

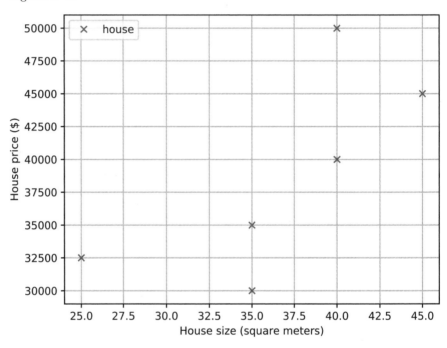

Figure 4-15: Housing data in the two-dimensional space

Can you see the general trend? With the growing size of your house, you can expect a linear growth of its market price. Double the square meters, and the price will double too.

In the code (see Listing 4-4), the client requests your price prediction for a house of 30 square meters. What does KNN with *k = 3* (in short, 3NN) predict? Take a look at Figure 4-16.

Beautiful, isn't it? The KNN algorithm finds the three closest houses with respect to house size and averages the predicted house price as the average of the *k=3* nearest neighbors. Thus, the result is $32,500.

If you are confused by the data conversions in the one-liner, let me quickly explain what is happening here:

```
KNN = KNeighborsRegressor(n_neighbors=3).fit(X[:,0].reshape(-1,1), X[:,1])
```

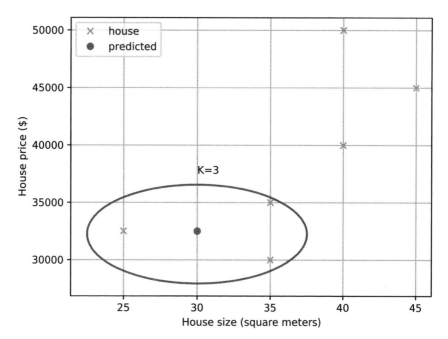

Figure 4-16: Housing data in the two-dimensional space with predicted house price for a new data point (house size equals 30 square meters) using KNN

First, you create a new machine learning model called KNeighborsRegressor. If you wanted to use KNN for classification, you'd use KNeighborsClassifier.

Second, you train the model by using the fit() function with two parameters. The first parameter defines the input (the house size), and the second parameter defines the output (the house price). The shape of both parameters must be an array-like data structure. For example, to use 30 as an input, you'd have to pass it as [30]. The reason is that, in general, the input can be multidimensional rather than one-dimensional. Therefore, you reshape the input:

```
print(X[:,0])
"[35 45 40 35 25 40]"


print(X[:,0].reshape(-1,1))
"""
[[35]
 [45]
 [40]
 [35]
 [25]
 [40]]
"""
```

Notice that if you were to use this 1D NumPy array as an input to the fit() function, the function wouldn't work because it expects an array of (array-like) observations, and not an array of integers.

In summary, this one-liner taught you how to create your first KNN regressor in a single line of code. If you have a lot of changing data and model updates, KNN is your best friend! Let's move on to a wildly popular machine learning model these days: neural networks.

Neural Network Analysis in One Line

Neural networks have gained massive popularity in recent years. This is in part because the algorithms and learning techniques in the field have improved, but also because of the improved hardware and the rise of general-purpose GPU (GPGPU) technology. In this section, you'll learn about the *multilayer perceptron (MLP)* which is one of the most popular neural network representations. After reading this, you'll be able to write your own neural network in a single line of Python code!

The Basics

For this one-liner, I have prepared a special data set with fellow Python colleagues on my email list. My goal was to create a relatable real-world data set, so I asked my email subscribers to participate in a data-generation experiment for this chapter.

The Data

If you're reading this book, you're interested in learning Python. To create an interesting data set, I asked my email subscribers six anonymized questions about their Python expertise and income. The responses to these questions will serve as training data for the simple neural network example (as a Python one-liner).

The training data is based on the answers to the following six questions:

- How many hours have you looked at Python code in the last seven days?
- How many years ago did you start to learn about computer science?
- How many coding books are on your shelf?
- What percentage of your Python time do you spend working on real-world projects?
- How much do you earn per month (round to $1000) from selling your technical skills (in the widest sense)?
- What's your approximate Finxter rating, rounded to 100 points?

The first five questions will be your input, and the sixth question will be the output for the neural network analysis. In this one-liner section, you're examining neural network regression. In other words, you predict a numerical value (your Python skills) based on numerical input features. We're not going to explore neural network classification in this book, which is another great strength of neural networks.

The sixth question approximates the skill level of a Python coder. Finxter (*https://finxter.com/*) is our puzzle-based learning application that assigns a rating value to any Python coder based on their performance in solving Python puzzles. In this way, it helps you quantify your skill level in Python.

Let's start with visualizing how each question influences the output (the skill rating of a Python developer), as shown in Figure 4-17.

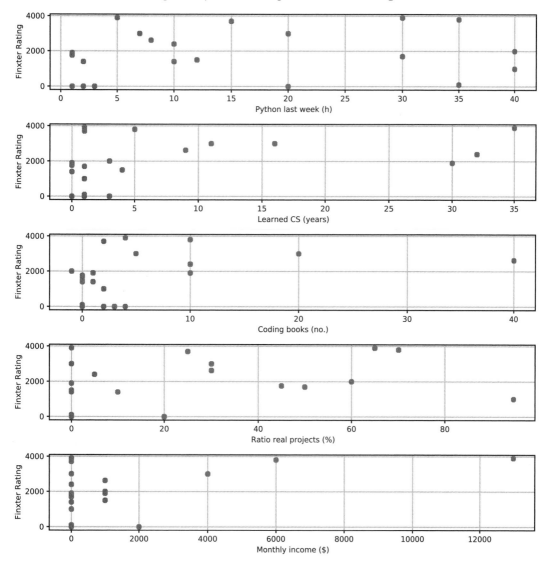

Figure 4-17: Relationship between questionnaire answers and the Python skill rating at Finxter

Note that these plots show only how each separate feature (question) impacts the final Finxter rating, but they tell you nothing about the impact of a combination of two or more features. Note also that some Pythonistas didn't answer all six questions; in those cases, I used the dummy value -1.

What Is an Artificial Neural Network?

The idea of creating a theoretical model of the human brain (the biological neural network) has been studied extensively in recent decades. But the foundations of artificial neural networks were proposed as early as the 1940s and '50s! Since then, the concept of artificial neural networks has been refined and continually improved.

The basic idea is to break the big task of learning and inference into multiple micro-tasks. These micro-tasks are not independent but interdependent. The brain consists of billions of neurons that are connected with trillions of synapses. In the simplified model, learning is merely adjusting the *strength* of synapses (also called *weights* or *parameters* in artificial neural networks). So how do you "create" a new synapse in the model? Simple— you increase its weight from zero to a nonzero value.

Figure 4-18 shows a basic neural network with three layers (input, hidden, output). Each layer consists of multiple neurons that are connected from the input layer via the hidden layer to the output layer.

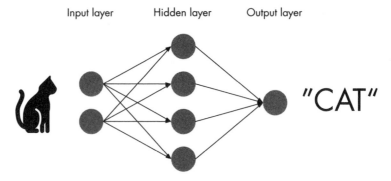

Figure 4-18: A simple neural network analysis for animal classification

In this example, the neural network is trained to detect animals in images. In practice, you would use one input neuron per pixel of the image as an input layer. This can result in millions of input neurons that are connected with millions of hidden neurons. Often, each output neuron is responsible for one bit of the overall output. For example, to detect two different animals (for example, cats and dogs), you'll use only a single neuron in the output layer that can model two different states (0=cat, 1=dog).

The idea is that each neuron can be activated, or "fired", when a certain input impulse arrives at the neuron. Each neuron decides independently, based on the strength of the input impulse, whether to fire or not. This way, you simulate the human brain, in which neurons activate each other via impulses. The activation of the input neurons propagates through the network until the output neurons are reached. Some output neurons will be activated, and others won't. The specific pattern of firing output neurons forms your final output (or prediction) of the artificial neural network. In your model, a firing output neuron could encode a 1, and a nonfiring output neuron could encode a 0. This way, you can train your neural network to predict anything that can be encoded as a series of 0s and 1s (which is everything a computer can represent).

Let's have a detailed look at how neurons work mathematically, in Figure 4-19.

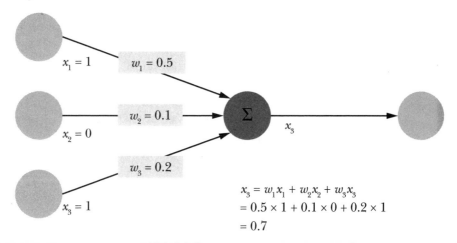

Figure 4-19: Mathematical model of a single neuron: the output is a function of the three inputs.

Each neuron is connected to other neurons, but not all connections are equal. Instead, each connection has an associated weight. Formally, a firing neuron propagates an impulse of 1 to the outgoing neighbors, while a non-firing neuron propagates an impulse of 0. You can think of the weight as indicating how much of the impulse of the firing input neuron is forwarded to the neuron via the connection. Mathematically, you multiply the impulse by the weight of the connection to calculate the input for the next neuron. In our example, the neuron simply sums over all inputs to calculate its own output. This is the *activation function* that describes how exactly the inputs of a neuron generate an output. In our example, a neuron fires with higher likelihood if its relevant input neurons fire too. This is how the impulses propagate through the neural network.

What does the learning algorithm do? It uses the training data to select the weights *w* of the neural network. Given a training input value *x*, different weights *w* lead to different outputs. Hence, the learning algorithm gradually changes the weights *w*—in many iterations—until the output layer produces similar results as the training data. In other words, the training algorithm gradually reduces the error of correctly predicting the training data.

There are many network structures, training algorithms, and activation functions. This chapter shows you a hands-on approach of using the neural network now, within a single line of code. You can then learn the finer details as you need to improve upon this (for example, you could start by reading the "Neural Network" entry on Wikipedia, *https://en.wikipedia.org /wiki/Neural_network*).

The Code

The goal is to create a neural network that predicts the Python skill level (Finxter rating) by using the five input features (answers to the questions):

WEEK How many hours have you been exposed to Python code in the last seven days?

YEARS How many years ago did you start to learn about computer science?

BOOKS How many coding books are on your shelf?

PROJECTS What percentage of your Python time do you spend implementing real-world projects?

EARN How much do you earn per month (round to $1000) from selling your technical skills (in the widest sense)?

Again, let's stand on the shoulders of giants and use the scikit-learn (sklearn) library for neural network regression, as in Listing 4-5.

```
## Dependencies
from sklearn.neural_network import MLPRegressor
import numpy as np

## Questionaire data (WEEK, YEARS, BOOKS, PROJECTS, EARN, RATING)
X = np.array(
    [[20,  11,  20,  30,  4000,  3000],
     [12,   4,   0,   0,  1000,  1500],
     [2,    0,   1,  10,     0,  1400],
     [35,   5,  10,  70,  6000,  3800],
     [30,   1,   4,  65,     0,  3900],
     [35,   1,   0,   0,     0,   100],
     [15,   1,   2,  25,     0,  3700],
     [40,   3,  -1,  60,  1000,  2000],
     [40,   1,   2,  95,     0,  1000],
     [10,   0,   0,   0,     0,  1400],
     [30,   1,   0,  50,     0,  1700],
     [1,    0,   0,  45,     0,  1762],
     [10,  32,  10,   5,     0,  2400],
     [5,   35,   4,   0, 13000,  3900],
     [8,    9,  40,  30,  1000,  2625],
     [1,    0,   1,   0,     0,  1900],
     [1,   30,  10,   0,  1000,  1900],
     [7,   16,   5,   0,     0,  3000]])

## One-liner
neural_net = MLPRegressor(max_iter=10000).fit(X[:,:-1], X[:,-1])

## Result
res = neural_net.predict([[0, 0, 0, 0, 0]])
print(res)
```

Listing 4-5: Neural network analysis in a single line of code

It's impossible for a human to correctly figure out the output—but would you like to try?

How It Works

In the first few lines, you create the data set. The machine learning algorithms in the scikit-learn library use a similar input format. Each row is a single observation with multiple features. The more rows, the more training data exists; the more columns, the more features of each observation. In this case, you have five features for the input and one feature for the output value of each training data.

The one-liner creates a neural network by using the constructor of the `MLPRegressor` class. I passed `max_iter=10000` as an argument because the training doesn't converge when using the default number of iterations (`max_iter=200`).

After that, you call the `fit()` function, which determines the parameters of the neural network. After calling `fit()`, the neural network has been successfully initialized. The `fit()` function takes a multidimensional input array (one observation per row, one feature per column) and a one-dimensional output array (size = number of observations).

The only thing left is calling the predict function on some input values:

```
## Result
res = neural_net.predict([[0, 0, 0, 0, 0]])
print(res)
# [94.94925927]
```

Note that the actual output may vary slightly because of the nondeterministic nature of the function and the different convergence behavior.

In plain English: if . . .

- . . . you have trained 0 hours in the last week,
- . . . you started your computer science studies 0 years ago,
- . . . you have 0 coding books in your shelf,
- . . . you spend 0 percent of your time implementing real Python projects, and
- . . . you earn $0 selling your coding skills,

the neural network estimates that your skill level is *very* low (a Finxter rating of 94 means you have difficulty understanding the Python program `print("hello, world")`).

So let's change this: what happens if you invest 20 hours a week learning and revisit the neural network after one week:

```
## Result
res = neural_net.predict([[20, 0, 0, 0, 0]])
print(res)
# [440.40167562]
```

Not bad—your skills improve quite significantly! But you're still not happy with this rating number, are you? (An above-average Python coder has at least a 1500–1700 rating on Finxter.)

No problem. Buy 10 Python books (only nine left after this one). Let's see what happens to your rating:

```
## Result
res = neural_net.predict([[20, 0, 10, 0, 0]])
print(res)
# [953.6317602]
```

Again, you make significant progress and double your rating number! But buying Python books alone will not help you much. You need to study them! Let's do this for a year:

```
## Result
res = neural_net.predict([[20, 1, 10, 0, 0]])
print(res)
# [999.94308353]
```

Not much happens. This is where I don't trust the neural network too much. In my opinion, you should have reached a much better performance of at least 1500. But this also shows that the neural network can be only as good as its training data. You have very limited data, and the neural network can't really overcome this limitation: there's just too little knowledge in a handful of data points.

But you don't give up, right? Next, you spend 50 percent of your Python time selling your skills as a Python freelancer:

```
## Result
res = neural_net.predict([[20, 1, 10, 50, 1000]])
print(res)
# [1960.7595547]
```

Boom! Suddenly the neural network considers you to be an expert Python coder. A wise prediction of the neural network, indeed! Learn Python for at least a year and do practical projects, and you'll become a great coder.

To sum up, you've learned about the basics of neural networks and how to use them in a single line of Python code. Interestingly, the questionnaire data indicates that starting out with practical projects—maybe even doing freelance projects from the beginning—matters a lot to your learning success. The neural network certainly knows that. If you want to learn my exact strategy of becoming a freelancer, join the free webinar about state-of-the-art Python freelancing at *https://blog.finxter.com/webinar-freelancer/*.

In the next section, you'll dive deeper into another powerful model representation: decision trees. While neural networks can be quite expensive to train (they often need multiple machines and many hours, and sometimes even weeks, to train), decision trees are lightweight. Nevertheless, they are a fast, effective way to extract patterns from your training data.

Decision-Tree Learning in One Line

Decision trees are powerful and intuitive tools in your machine learning tool-belt. A big advantage of decision trees is that, unlike many other machine learning techniques, they're human-readable. You can easily train a decision tree and show it to your supervisors, who do not need to know anything about machine learning in order to understand what your model does. This is especially great for data scientists who often must defend and present their results to management. In this section, I'll show you how to use decision trees in a single line of Python code.

The Basics

Unlike many machine learning algorithms, the ideas behind decision trees might be familiar from your own experience. They represent a structured way of making decisions. Each decision opens new branches. By answering a bunch of questions, you'll finally land on the recommended outcome. Figure 4-20 shows an example.

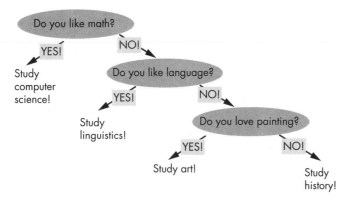

Figure 4-20: A simplified decision tree for recommending a study subject

Decision trees are used for classification problems such as "which subject should I study, given my interests?" You start at the top. Now, you repeatedly answer questions and select the choices that describe your features best. Finally, you reach a *leaf node* of the tree, a node with no *children*. This is the recommended class based on your feature selection.

Decision-tree learning has many nuances. In the preceding example, the first question carries more weight than the last question. If you like math, the decision tree will never recommend art or linguistics. This is useful because some features may be much more important for the classification decision than others. For example, a classification system that predicts your current health may use your sex (feature) to practically rule out many diseases (classes).

Hence, the order of the decision nodes lends itself to performance optimizations: place the features at the top that have a high impact on the final classification. In decision-tree learning, you'll then aggregate the questions with little impact on the final classification, as shown in Figure 4-21.

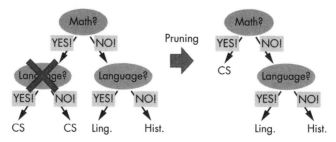

Figure 4-21: Pruning improves efficiency of decision-tree learning.

Suppose the full decision tree looks like the tree on the left. For any combination of features, there's a separate classification outcome (the tree leaves). However, some features may not give you any additional information with respect to the classification problem (for example, the first Language decision node in the example). Decision-tree learning would effectively get rid of these nodes for efficiency reasons, a process called *pruning*.

The Code

You can create your own decision tree in a single line of Python code. Listing 4-6 shows you how.

```
## Dependencies
from sklearn import tree
import numpy as np


## Data: student scores in (math, language, creativity) --> study field
X = np.array([[9, 5, 6, "computer science"],
              [1, 8, 1, "linguistics"],
              [5, 7, 9, "art"]])


## One-liner
Tree = tree.DecisionTreeClassifier().fit(X[:,:-1], X[:,-1])

## Result & puzzle
student_0 = Tree.predict([[8, 6, 5]])
print(student_0)

student_1 = Tree.predict([[3, 7, 9]])
print(student_1)
```

Listing 4-6: Decision-tree classification in a single line of code

Guess the output of this code snippet!

How It Works

The data in this code describes three students with their estimated skill levels (a score from 1–10) in the three areas of math, language, and creativity. You also know the study subjects of these students. For example, the first student is highly skilled in math and studies computer science. The second student is skilled in language much more than in the other two skills and studies linguistics. The third student is skilled in creativity and studies art.

The one-liner creates a new decision-tree object and trains the model by using the fit() function on the labeled training data (the last column is the label). Internally, it creates three nodes, one for each feature: math, language, and creativity. When predicting the class of student_0 (math = 8, language = 6, creativity = 5), the decision tree returns computer science. It has learned that this feature pattern (high, medium, medium) is an indicator of the first class. On the other hand, when asked for (3, 7, 9), the decision tree predicts art because it has learned that the score (low, medium, high) hints to the third class.

Note that the algorithm is nondeterministic. In other words, when executing the same code twice, different results may arise. This is common for machine learning algorithms that work with random generators. In this case, the order of the features is randomly organized, so the final decision tree may have a different order of the features.

To summarize, decision trees are an intuitive way of creating human-readable machine learning models. Every branch represents a choice based on a single feature of a new sample. The leaves of the tree represent the final prediction (classification or regression). Next, we'll leave concrete machine learning algorithms for a moment and explore a critical concept in machine learning: variance.

Get Row with Minimal Variance in One Line

You may have read about the Vs in Big Data: volume, velocity, variety, veracity, and value. *Variance* is yet another important V: it measures the expected (squared) deviation of the data from its mean. In practice, variance is an important measure with relevant application domains in financial services, weather forecasting, and image processing.

The Basics

Variance measures how much data spreads around its average in the one-dimensional or multidimensional space. You'll see a graphical example in a moment. In fact, variance is one of the most important properties in machine learning. It captures the patterns of the data in a generalized manner—and machine learning is all about pattern recognition.

Many machine learning algorithms rely on variance in one form or another. For instance, the *bias-variance trade-off* is a well-known problem in machine learning: sophisticated machine learning models risk overfitting the data (high variance) but represent the training data very accurately (low bias). On the other hand, simple models often generalize well (low variance) but do not represent the data accurately (high bias).

So what exactly is variance? It's a simple statistical property that captures how much the data set spreads from its mean. Figure 4-22 shows an example plotting two data sets: one with low variance, and one with high variance.

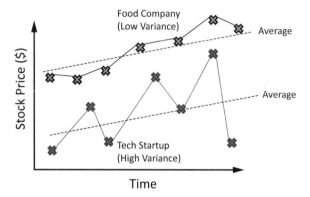

Figure 4-22: Variance comparison of two company stock prices

This example shows the stock prices of two companies. The stock price of the tech startup fluctuates heavily around its average. The stock price of the food company is quite stable and fluctuates only in minor ways around the average. In other words, the tech startup has high variance, and the food company has low variance.

In mathematical terms, you can calculate the variance $var(X)$ of a set of numerical values X by using the following formula:

$$var(X) = \sum_{x \in X} (x - \bar{x})^2$$

The value $\bar{x}$ is the average value of the data in X.

The Code

As they get older, many investors want to reduce the overall risk of their investment portfolio. According to the dominant investment philosophy, you should consider stocks with lower variance as less-risky investment vehicles. Roughly speaking, you can lose less money investing in a stable, predictable, and large company than in a small tech startup.

The goal of the one-liner in Listing 4-7 is to identify the stock in your portfolio with minimal variance. By investing more money into this stock, you can expect a lower overall variance of your portfolio.

```
## Dependencies
import numpy as np

## Data (rows: stocks / cols: stock prices)
X = np.array([[25,27,29,30],
              [1,5,3,2],
              [12,11,8,3],
              [1,1,2,2],
              [2,6,2,2]])


## One-liner
# Find the stock with smallest variance
min_row = min([(i,np.var(X[i,:])) for i in range(len(X))], key=lambda x: x[1])


## Result & puzzle
print("Row with minimum variance: " + str(min_row[0]))
print("Variance: " + str(min_row[1]))
```

Listing 4-7: Calculating minimum variance in a single line of code

What's the output of this code snippet?

How It Works

As usual, you first define the data you want to run the one-liner on (see the top of Listing 4-7). The NumPy array X contains five rows (one row per stock in your portfolio) with four values per row (stock prices).

The goal is to find the ID and variance of the stock with minimal variance. Hence, the outermost function of the one-liner is the min() function. You execute the min() function on a sequence of tuples (a,b), where the first tuple value a is the row index (stock index), and the second tuple value b is the variance of the row.

You may ask: what's the minimal value of a sequence of tuples? Of course, you need to properly define this operation before using it. To this end, you use the key argument of the min() function. The key argument takes a function that returns a comparable object value, given a sequence value. Again, our sequence values are tuples, and you need to find the tuple with minimal variance (the second tuple value). Because variance is the second value, you'll return x[1] as the basis for comparison. In other words, the tuple with the minimal second tuple value wins.

Let's look at how to create the sequence of tuple values. You use list comprehension to create a tuple for any row index (stock). The first tuple element is simply the index of row *i*. The second tuple element is the variance of this row. You use the NumPy var() function in combination with slicing to calculate the row variance.

The result of the one-liner is, therefore, as follows:

```
"""
Row with minimum variance: 3
Variance: 0.25
"""
```

I'd like to add that there's an alternative way of solving this problem. If this wasn't a book about Python one-liners, I would prefer the following solution instead of the one-liner:

```
var = np.var(X, axis=1)
min_row = (np.where(var==min(var)), min(var))
```

In the first line, you calculate the variance of the NumPy array X along the columns (axis=1). In the second line, you create the tuple. The first tuple value is the index of the minimum in the variance array. The second tuple value is the minimum in the variance array. Note that multiple rows may have the same (minimal) variance.

This solution is more readable. So clearly, there is a trade-off between conciseness and readability. Just because you can cram everything into a single line of code doesn't mean you should. All things being equal, it's much better to write concise *and* readable code, instead of blowing up your code with unnecessary definitions, comments, or intermediate steps.

After learning the basics of variance in this section, you're now ready to absorb how to calculate basic statistics.

Basic Statistics in One Line

As a data scientist and machine learning engineer, you need to know basic statistics. Some machine learning algorithms are entirely based on statistics (for example, Bayesian networks).

For example, extracting basic statistics from matrices (such as average, variance, and standard deviation) is a critical component for analyzing a wide range of data sets such as financial data, health data, or social media data. With the rise of machine learning and data science, knowing about how to use NumPy—which is at the heart of Python data science, statistics, and linear algebra—will become more and more valuable to the marketplace.

In this one-liner, you'll learn how to calculate basic statistics with NumPy.

The Basics

This section explains how to calculate the average, the standard deviation, and the variance along an axis. These three calculations are very similar; if you understand one, you'll understand all of them.

Here's what you want to achieve: given a NumPy array of stock data with rows indicating the different companies and columns indicating their daily stock prices, the goal is to find the average and standard deviation of each company's stock price (see Figure 4-23).

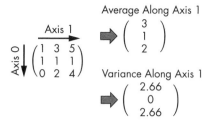

Figure 4-23: Average and variance along axis 1

This example shows a two-dimensional NumPy array, but in practice, the array can have much higher dimensionality.

Simple Average, Variance, Standard Deviation

Before examining how to accomplish this in NumPy, let's slowly build the background you need to know. Say you want to calculate the simple average, the variance, or the standard deviation over all values in a NumPy array. You've already seen examples of the average and the variance function in this chapter. The standard deviation is simply the square root of the variance. You can achieve this easily with the following functions:

```
import numpy as np

X = np.array([[1, 3, 5],
              [1, 1, 1],
              [0, 2, 4]])



print(np.average(X))
# 2.0

print(np.var(X))
# 2.4444444444444446

print(np.std(X))
# 1.5634719199411433
```

You may have noted that you apply those functions on the two-dimensional NumPy array X. But NumPy simply flattens the array and calculates the functions on the flattened array. For example, the simple average of the flattened NumPy array X is calculated as follows:

$$(1 + 3 + 5 + 1 + 1 + 1 + 0 + 2 + 4) / 9 = 18 / 9 = 2.0$$

Calculating Average, Variance, Standard Deviation Along an Axis

However, sometimes you want to calculate these functions along an axis. You can do this by specifying the keyword axis as an argument to the average, variance, and standard deviation functions (see Chapter 3 for a detailed introduction to the axis argument).

The Code

Listing 4-8 shows you exactly how to calculate the average, variance, and standard deviation along an axis. Our goal is to calculate the averages, variances, and standard deviations of all stocks in a two-dimensional matrix with rows representing stocks and columns representing daily prices.

```
## Dependencies
import numpy as np


## Stock Price Data: 5 companies
# (row=[price_day_1, price_day_2, ...])
x = np.array([[8, 9, 11, 12],
              [1, 2, 2, 1],
              [2, 8, 9, 9],
              [9, 6, 6, 3],
              [3, 3, 3, 3]])


## One-liner
avg, var, std = np.average(x, axis=1), np.var(x, axis=1), np.std(x, axis=1)


## Result & puzzle
print("Averages: " + str(avg))
print("Variances: " + str(var))
print("Standard Deviations: " + str(std))
```

Listing 4-8: Calculating basic statistics along an axis

Guess the output of the puzzle!

How It Works

The one-liner uses the axis keyword to specify the axis along which to calculate the average, variance, and standard deviation. For example, if you perform these three functions along axis=1, each row is aggregated into a single value. Hence, the resulting NumPy array has a reduced dimensionality of one.

The result of the puzzle is the following:

```
"""
Averages: [10.   1.5  7.   6.   3. ]
Variances: [2.5  0.25 8.5  4.5  0. ]
Standard Deviations: [1.58113883 0.5    2.91547595 2.12132034 0.   ]
"""
```

Before moving on to the next one-liner, I want to show you how to use the same idea for an even higher-dimensional NumPy array.

When averaging along an axis for high-dimensional NumPy arrays, you'll always aggregate the axis defined in the axis argument. Here's an example:

```
import numpy as np

x = np.array([[[1,2], [1,1]],
              [[1,1], [2,1]],
              [[1,0], [0,0]]])


print(np.average(x, axis=2))
print(np.var(x, axis=2))
print(np.std(x, axis=2))

"""
[[1.5 1. ]
 [1.  1.5]
 [0.5 0. ]]
[[0.25 0.  ]
 [0.   0.25]
 [0.25 0.  ]]
[[0.5 0. ]
 [0.  0.5]
 [0.5 0. ]]
"""
```

There are three examples of computing the average, variance, and standard deviation along axis 2 (see Chapter 3; the innermost axis). In other words, all values of axis 2 will be combined into a single value that results in axis 2 being dropped from the resulting array. Dive into the three examples and figure out how exactly axis 2 is collapsed into a single average, variance, or standard deviation value.

To summarize, a wide range of data sets (including financial data, health data, and social media data) requires you to be able to extract basic insights from your data sets. This section gives you a deeper understanding of how to use the powerful NumPy toolset to extract basic statistics quickly and efficiently from multidimensional arrays. This is needed as a basic pre-processing step for many machine learning algorithms.

Classification with Support-Vector Machines in One Line

Support-vector machines (*SVMs*) have gained massive popularity in recent years because they have robust classification performance, even in high-dimensional spaces. Surprisingly, SVMs work even if there are more dimensions (features) than data items. This is unusual for classification algorithms because of the *curse of dimensionality*: with increasing dimensionality, the data becomes extremely sparse, which makes it hard for algorithms to find patterns in the data set. Understanding the basic ideas of SVMs is a fundamental step to becoming a sophisticated machine learning engineer.

The Basics

How do classification algorithms work? They use the training data to find a decision boundary that divides data in the one class from data in the other class (in "Logistic Regression in One Line" on page 89, the decision boundary would be whether the probability of the sigmoid function is below or above the 0.5 threshold).

A High-Level Look at Classification

Figure 4-24 shows an example of a general classifier.

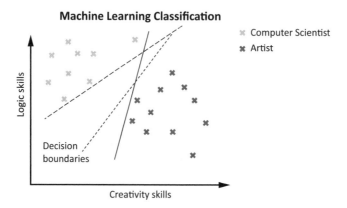

Figure 4-24: Diverse skill sets of computer scientists and artists

Suppose you want to build a recommendation system for aspiring university students. The figure visualizes the training data consisting of users classified according to their skills in two areas: logic and creativity. Some people have high logic skills and relatively low creativity; others have high creativity and relatively low logic skills. The first group is labeled as *computer scientists*, and the second group is labeled as *artists*.

To classify new users, the machine learning model must find a decision boundary that separates the computer scientists from the artists. Roughly speaking, you'll classify a user by where they fall with respect to the decision boundary. In the example, you'll classify users who fall into the left area as computer scientists, and users who fall into the right area as artists.

In the two-dimensional space, the decision boundary is either a line or a (higher-order) curve. The former is called a *linear classifier*, and the latter is called a *nonlinear classifier*. In this section, we'll explore only linear classifiers.

Figure 4-24 shows three decision boundaries that are all valid separators of the data. In our example, it's impossible to quantify which of the given decision boundaries is better; they all lead to perfect accuracy when classifying the training data.

But What Is the Best Decision Boundary?

Support-vector machines provide a unique and beautiful answer to this question. Arguably, the best decision boundary provides a maximal margin of safety. In other words, SVMs maximize the distance between the closest data points and the decision boundary. The goal is to minimize the error of new points that are close to the decision boundary.

Figure 4-25 shows an example.

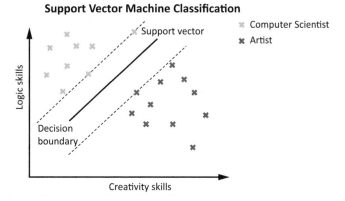

Figure 4-25: Support-vector machines maximize the error of margin.

The SVM classifier finds the respective support vectors so that the zone between the support vectors is as thick as possible. Here, the support vectors are the data points that lie on the two dotted lines parallel to the decision boundary. These lines are denoted as *margins*. The decision boundary is the line in the middle with maximal distance to the margins. Because the zone between the margins and the decision boundary is maximized, the *margin of error* is expected to be maximal when classifying new data points. This idea shows high classification accuracy for many practical problems.

The Code

Is it possible to create your own SVM in a single line of Python code? Take a look at Listing 4-9.

```
## Dependencies
from sklearn import svm
import numpy as np


## Data: student scores in (math, language, creativity) --> study field
X = np.array([[9, 5, 6, "computer science"],
              [10, 1, 2, "computer science"],
              [1, 8, 1, "literature"],
              [4, 9, 3, "literature"],
              [0, 1, 10, "art"],
              [5, 7, 9, "art"]])
```

```
## One-liner
svm = svm.SVC().fit(X[:,:-1], X[:,-1])


## Result & puzzle
student_0 = svm.predict([[3, 3, 6]])
print(student_0)

student_1 = svm.predict([[8, 1, 1]])
print(student_1)
```

Listing 4-9: SVM classification in a single line of code

Guess the output of this code.

How It Works

The code breaks down how you can use support-vector machines in Python in the most basic form. The NumPy array holds the labeled training data with one row per user and one column per feature (skill level in math, language, and creativity). The last column is the label (the class).

Because you have three-dimensional data, the support-vector machine separates the data by using two-dimensional planes (the linear separator) rather than one-dimensional lines. As you can see, it's also possible to separate three classes rather than only two as shown in the preceding examples.

The one-liner itself is straightforward: you first create the model by using the constructor of the svm.SVC class (*SVC* stands for *support-vector classification*). Then, you call the fit() function to perform the training based on your labeled training data.

In the results part of the code snippet, you call the predict() function on new observations. Because student_0 has skills indicated as math=3, language=3, and creativity=6, the support-vector machine predicts that the label *art* fits this student's skills. Similarly, student_1 has skills indicated as math=8, language=1, and creativity=1. Thus, the support-vector machine predicts that the label *computer science* fits this student's skills.

Here's the final output of the one-liner:

```
## Result & puzzle
student_0 = svm.predict([[3, 3, 6]])
print(student_0)
# ['art']

student_1 = svm.predict([[8, 1, 1]])
print(student_1)
## ['computer science']
```

In summary, SVMs perform well even in high-dimensional spaces when there are more features than training data vectors. The idea of maximizing the *margin of safety* is intuitive and leads to robust performance when classifying *boundary cases*—that is, vectors that fall within the margin of safety. In the final section of this chapter, we'll zoom one step back and have a look at a meta-algorithm for classification: ensemble learning with random forests.

Classification with Random Forests in One Line

Let's move on to an exciting machine learning technique: *ensemble learning*. Here's my quick-and-dirty tip if your prediction accuracy is lacking but you need to meet the deadline at all costs: try this meta-learning approach that combines the predictions (or classifications) of multiple machine learning algorithms. In many cases, it will give you better last-minute results.

The Basics

In the previous sections, you've studied multiple machine learning algorithms that you can use to get quick results. However, different algorithms have different strengths. For example, neural network classifiers can generate excellent results for complex problems. However, they are also prone to overfitting the data because of their powerful capacity to memorize fine-grained patterns of the data. Ensemble learning for classification problems partially overcomes the problem that you often don't know in advance which machine learning technique works best.

How does this work? You create a meta-classifier consisting of multiple types or instances of basic machine learning algorithms. In other words, you train multiple models. To classify a single observation, you ask all models to classify the input independently. Next, you return the class that was returned most often, given your input, as a *meta-prediction*. This is the final output of your ensemble learning algorithm.

Random forests are a special type of ensemble learning algorithms. They focus on decision-tree learning. A forest consists of many trees. Similarly, a random forest consists of many decision trees. Each decision tree is built by injecting randomness in the tree-generation procedure during the training phase (for example, which tree node to select first). This leads to various decision trees—exactly what you want.

Figure 4-26 shows how the prediction works for a trained random forest using the following scenario. Alice has high math and language skills. The *ensemble* consists of three decision trees (building a random forest). To classify Alice, each decision tree is queried about Alice's classification. Two of the decision trees classify Alice as a computer scientist. Because this is the class with the most votes, it's returned as the final output for the classification.

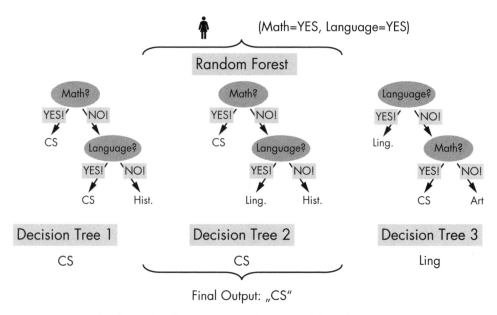

Figure 4-26: Random forest classifier aggregating the output of three decision trees

The Code

Let's stick to this example of classifying the study field based on a student's skill level in three areas (math, language, creativity). You may think that implementing an ensemble learning method is complicated in Python. But it's not, thanks to the comprehensive scikit-learn library (see Listing 4-10).

```
## Dependencies
import numpy as np
from sklearn.ensemble import RandomForestClassifier
```

```
## Data: student scores in (math, language, creativity) --> study field
X = np.array([[9, 5, 6, "computer science"],
              [5, 1, 5, "computer science"],
              [8, 8, 8, "computer science"],
              [1, 10, 7, "literature"],
              [1, 8, 1, "literature"],
              [5, 7, 9, "art"],
              [1, 1, 6, "art"]])
```

```
## One-liner
Forest = RandomForestClassifier(n_estimators=10).fit(X[:,:-1], X[:,-1])
```

```
## Result
students = Forest.predict([[8, 6, 5],
                           [3, 7, 9],
                           [2, 2, 1]])
print(students)
```

Listing 4-10: Ensemble learning with random forest classifiers

Take a guess: what's the output of this code snippet?

How It Works

After initializing the labeled training data in Listing 4-10, the code creates a random forest by using the constructor on the class RandomForestClassifier with one parameter n_estimators that defines the number of trees in the forest. Next, you populate the model that results from the previous initialization (an empty forest) by calling the function fit(). To this end, the input training data consists of all but the last column of array X, while the labels of the training data are defined in the last column. As in the previous examples, you use slicing to extract the respective columns from the data array X.

The classification part is slightly different in this code snippet. I wanted to show you how to classify multiple observations instead of only one. You can achieve this here by creating a multidimensional array with one row per observation.

Here's the output of the code snippet:

```
## Result
students = Forest.predict([[8, 6, 5],
                           [3, 7, 9],
                           [2, 2, 1]])
print(students)
# ['computer science' 'art' 'art']
```

Note that the result is still nondeterministic (the result may be different for different executions of the code) because the random forest algorithm relies on the random number generator that returns different numbers at different points in time. You can make this call deterministic by using the integer argument random_state. For example, you can set random_state=1 when calling the random forest constructor: RandomForestClassifier(n_estimators=10, random_state=1). In this case, each time you create a new random forest classifier, the same output results because the same random numbers are created: they are all based on the seed integer 1.

In summary, this section introduced a meta-approach for classification: using the output of various decision trees to reduce the variance of the classification error. This is one version of ensemble learning, which combines multiple basic models into a single meta-model that's able to leverage their individual strengths.

NOTE   *Two different decision trees can lead to a high variance of the error: one generates good results, while the other one doesn't. By using random forests, you mitigate this effect.*

Variations of this idea are common in machine learning—and if you need to quickly improve your prediction accuracy, simply run multiple machine learning models and evaluate their output to find the best one (a quick-and-dirty secret of machine learning practitioners). In a way, ensemble learning techniques automatically perform the task that's often done by experts in practical machine learning pipelines: selecting, comparing, and combining the output of different machine learning models. The big strength of ensemble learning is that this can be done individually for each data value at runtime.

Summary

This chapter covered 10 basic machine learning algorithms that are fundamental to your success in the field. You've learned about regression algorithms to predict values such as linear regression, KNNs, and neural networks. You've learned about classification algorithms such as logistic regression, decision-tree learning, SVMs, and random forests. Furthermore, you've learned how to calculate basic statistics of multidimensional data arrays, and to use the K-Means algorithm for unsupervised learning. These algorithms and methods are among the most important algorithms in the field of machine learning, and there are a lot more to study if you want to start working as a machine learning engineer. That learning will pay off—machine learning engineers usually earn six figures in the United States (a simple web search should confirm this)! For students who want to dive deeper into machine learning, I recommend the excellent (and free) Coursera course from Andrew Ng. You can find the course material online by asking your favorite search engine.

In the next chapter, you'll study one of the most important (and most undervalued) skills of highly efficient programmers: regular expressions. While this chapter was a bit more on the conceptual side (you learned the general ideas, but the scikit-learn library did the heavy lifting), the next chapter will be highly technical. So, roll up your sleeves and read on!

5

REGULAR EXPRESSIONS

Are you an office worker, student, software developer, manager, blogger, researcher, author, copywriter, teacher, or self-employed freelancer? Most likely, you're spending many hours in front of your computer, day after day. Improving your daily productivity—only by a small fraction of a percentage—will mean a gain of thousands, if not tens of thousands, of dollars of productivity and hundreds of hours of additional free time over the years.

This chapter shows you an undervalued technique that helps master coders be more efficient when working with textual data: using regular expressions. This chapter shows you 10 ways of using regular expressions to solve everyday problems with less effort, time, and energy. Study this chapter about regular expressions carefully—it'll be worth your time!

Finding Basic Textual Patterns in Strings

This section introduces regular expressions using the re module and its important re.findall() function. I'll start by explaining several basic regular expressions.

The Basics

A *regular expression* (*regex*, for short) formally describes a search *pattern* that you can use to match sections of text. The simple example in Figure 5-1 shows a search of Shakespeare's text *Romeo and Juliet* for the pattern Juliet.

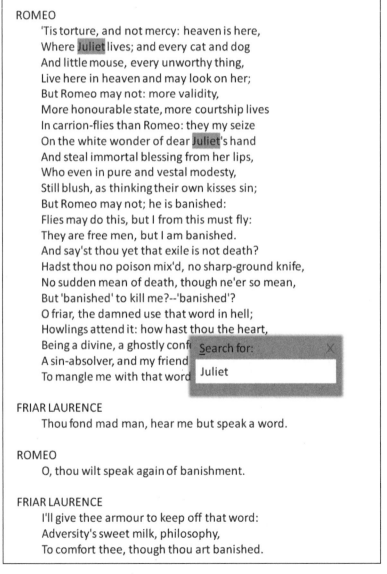

ROMEO
    'Tis torture, and not mercy: heaven is here,
    Where Juliet lives; and every cat and dog
    And little mouse, every unworthy thing,
    Live here in heaven and may look on her;
    But Romeo may not: more validity,
    More honourable state, more courtship lives
    In carrion-flies than Romeo: they my seize
    On the white wonder of dear Juliet's hand
    And steal immortal blessing from her lips,
    Who even in pure and vestal modesty,
    Still blush, as thinking their own kisses sin;
    But Romeo may not; he is banished:
    Flies may do this, but I from this must fly:
    They are free men, but I am banished.
    And say'st thou yet that exile is not death?
    Hadst thou no poison mix'd, no sharp-ground knife,
    No sudden mean of death, though ne'er so mean,
    But 'banished' to kill me?--'banished'?
    O friar, the damned use that word in hell;
    Howlings attend it: how hast thou the heart,
    Being a divine, a ghostly conf[Search for:
    A sin-absolver, and my friend
    To mangle me with that word   Juliet

FRIAR LAURENCE
    Thou fond mad man, hear me but speak a word.

ROMEO
    O, thou wilt speak again of banishment.

FRIAR LAURENCE
    I'll give thee armour to keep off that word:
    Adversity's sweet milk, philosophy,
    To comfort thee, though thou art banished.

Figure 5-1: Searching Shakespeare's Romeo and Juliet *for the pattern* Juliet

Figure 5-1 shows that the most basic regular expression is a simple string pattern. The string 'Juliet' is a perfectly valid regular expression.

Regular expressions are incredibly powerful, and can do much more than regular text search, but they're built using only a handful of basic commands. Learn these basic commands and you'll be able to understand and write complex regular expressions. In this section, we'll focus on the three most important regex commands that extend the functionality of simple search of string patterns in a given text.

The Dot Regex

First, you need to know how to match an arbitrary character by using the *dot regex*, the . character. The dot regex matches any character (including whitespace characters). You can use it to indicate that you don't care which character matches, as long as *exactly one* matches:

```
import re

text = '''A blockchain, originally block chain,
is a growing list of records, called blocks,
which are linked using cryptography.
'''

print(re.findall('b...k', text))
# ['block', 'block', 'block']
```

This example uses the findall() method of the re module. The first argument is the regex itself: you search for any string pattern starting with the character 'b', followed by three arbitrary characters, ... , followed by the character 'k'. This regex b...k matches the word 'block' but also 'boook', 'b erk', and 'bloek'. The second parameter to findall() is the text you're searching. The string variable text contains three matching patterns, as you can see in the output of the print statement.

The Asterisk Regex

Second, say you want to match text that begins and ends with the character 'y' and an arbitrary number of characters in between. How do you accomplish this? You can do by this using the *asterisk regex*, the * character. Unlike the dot regex, the asterisk regex can't stand on its own; it modifies the meaning of another regex. Consider the following example:

```
print(re.findall('y.*y', text))
# ['yptography']
```

The asterisk operator applies to the regex immediately in front of it. In this example, the regex pattern starts with the character 'y', followed by an arbitrary number of characters, .*, followed by the character 'y'. As you can see, the word 'cryptography' contains one such instance of this pattern: 'yptography'.

You may wonder why this code doesn't find the long substring between 'originally' and 'cryptography', which should also match the regex pattern y.*y. The reason is simply that the dot operator matches any character except the newline character. The string stored in the variable text is a multiline string with three new lines. You can also use the asterisk operator in combination with any other regex. For example, you can use the regex abc* to match the strings 'ab', 'abc', 'abcc', and 'abccdc'.

The Zero-or-one Regex

Third, you need to know how to match zero or one characters by using the *zero-or-one regex*, the ? character. Just like the asterisk operator, the question mark modifies another regex, as you can see in the following example:

```
print(re.findall('blocks?', text))
# ['block', 'block', 'blocks']
```

The zero-or-one regex, ?, applies to the regex immediately in front of it. In our case, this is the character s. The zero-or-one regex says that the pattern it modifies is optional.

There is another use of the question mark in Python's re package, but it has nothing to do with the zero-or-one regex: the question mark can be combined with the asterisk operator, *?, to allow for *nongreedy* pattern matching. For example, if you use the regex .*?, Python searches for a minimal number of arbitrary characters. In contrast, if you use the asterisk operator * without the question mark, it *greedily* matches as many characters as possible.

Let's look at an example. When searching the HTML string '<div>hello world</div>' by using the regex <.*>, it matches the whole string '<div>hello world</div>' rather than only the prefix '<div>'. If you want only the prefix, you can use the nongreedy regex <.*?>:

```
txt = '<div>hello world</div>'

print(re.findall('<.*>', txt))
# ['<div>hello world</div>']

print(re.findall('<.*?>', txt))
# ['<div>', '</div>']
```

Equipped with these three tools—the dot regex ., the asterisk regex *, and the zero-or-one regex ?—you're now able to comprehend the next one-liner solution.

The Code

Our input is a string, and our goal is to use a nongreedy approach to find all patterns that start with the character 'p', end with the character 'r', and have at least one occurrence of the character 'e' (and, possibly, an arbitrary number of other characters) in between!

These types of text queries occur quite frequently—especially in companies that focus on text processing, speech recognition, or machine translation (such as search engines, social networks, or video platforms). Take a look at Listing 5-1.

```
## Dependencies
import re


## Data
text = 'peter piper picked a peck of pickled peppers'


## One-Liner
result = re.findall('p.*?e.*?r', text)


## Result
print(result)
```

Listing 5-1: One-liner solution to search for specific phrases (nongreedy)

This code prints a list of all matching phrases in the text. What are they?

How It Works

The regex search query is p.*?e.*?r. Let's break this down. You're looking for a phrase that starts with the character 'p' and ends with the character 'r'. Between those two characters, you require one occurrence of the character 'e'. Apart from that, you allow an arbitrary number of characters (whitespace or not). However, you match in a nongreedy manner by using .*?, which means Python will search for a minimal number of arbitrary characters. Here's the solution:

```
## Result
print(result)
# ['peter', 'piper', 'picked a peck of pickled pepper']
```

Compare this solution with the one you'd get when using the greedy regex p.*e.*r:

```
result = re.findall('p.*e.*r', text)
print(result)
# ['peter piper picked a peck of pickled pepper']
```

The first greedy asterisk operator .* matches almost the whole string before it terminates.

Writing Your First Web Scraper with Regular Expressions

In the previous section, you learned about the most powerful way to find arbitrary text patterns in strings: regular expressions. This section will further motivate your use of regular expressions and develop your knowledge with a practical example.

The Basics

Suppose you're working as a freelance software developer. Your client is a fintech startup that needs to stay updated about the latest developments in cryptocurrency. They hire you to write a web scraper that regularly pulls the HTML source code of news websites and searches it for words starting with 'crypto' (for example, 'cryptocurrency', 'crypto-bot', 'crypto-crash', and so on).

Your first attempt is the following code snippet:

```
import urllib.request

search_phrase = 'crypto'

with urllib.request.urlopen('https://www.wired.com/') as response:
    html = response.read().decode("utf8") # convert to string
    first_pos = html.find(search_phrase)
    print(html[first_pos-10:first_pos+10])
```

The method urlopen() (from the module urllib.request) pulls the HTML source code from the specified URL. Because the result is a byte array, you have to first convert it to a string by using the decode() method. Then you use the string method find() to return the position of the first occurrence of the searched string. With slicing (see Chapter 2), you carve out a substring that returns the immediate environment of the position. The result is the following string:

```
# ,r=window.crypto||wi
```

Aw. That looks bad. As it turns out, the search phrase is ambiguous—most words containing 'crypto' are semantically unrelated to *cryptocurrencies*. Your web scraper generates *false positives* (it finds string results that you originally didn't mean to find). So how can you fix it?

Luckily, you've just read this Python book, so the answer is obvious: regular expressions! Your idea to remove false positives is to search for occurrences in which the word 'crypto' is followed by up to 30 arbitrary characters, followed by the word coin. Roughly speaking, the search query is crypto + *<up to 30 arbitrary characters>* + coin. Consider the following two examples:

- 'crypto-bot that is trading Bitcoin'—yes
- 'cryptographic encryption methods that can be cracked easily with quantum computers'—no

So how to solve this problem of allowing up to 30 arbitrary characters between two strings? This goes beyond a simple string search. You can't enumerate every exact string pattern—a virtually infinite number of matches is allowed. For example, the search pattern must match all of the following: `'cryptoxxxcoin'`, `'crypto coin'`, `'crypto bitcoin'`, `'crypto is a currency. Bitcoin'`, and all other character combinations with up to 30 characters between the two strings. Even if you had only 26 characters in the alphabet, the number of strings that would theoretically match our requirement exceeds 26^{30} = 2,813,198,901,284,745,919,258,621,029,615,971,520,741,376. In the following, you'll learn how to search a text for a regex pattern that corresponds to a large number of possible string patterns.

The Code

Here, given a string, you will find occurrences in which the string `'crypto'` is followed by up to 30 arbitrary characters, followed by the string `'coin'`. Let's first look at Listing 5-2 before discussing how the code solves the problem.

```
## Dependencies
import re


## Data
text_1 = "crypto-bot that is trading Bitcoin and other currencies"
text_2 = "cryptographic encryption methods that can be cracked easily with quantum computers"


## One-Liner
pattern = re.compile("crypto(.{1,30})coin")


## Result
print(pattern.match(text_1))
print(pattern.match(text_2))
```

Listing 5-2: One-liner solution to find text snippets in the form crypto(some text)coin

This code searches two string variables, text_1 and text_2. Does the search query (pattern) match them?

How It Works

First, you import the standard module for regular expressions in Python, called re. The important stuff happens in the one-liner where you compile the search query crypto(.{1,30})coin. This is the query that you can use to search various strings. You use the following special regex characters. Read them from top to bottom and you'll understand the meaning of the pattern in Listing 5-2:

- () matches whatever regex is inside.

- . matches an arbitrary character.

- {1,30} matches between 1 and 30 occurrences of the *previous* regex.

- (.{1,30}) matches between 1 and 30 arbitrary characters.

- crypto(.{1,30})coin matches the regex consisting of three parts: the word 'crypto', an arbitrary sequence with 1 to 30 chars, followed by the word 'coin'.

We say that the pattern is *compiled* because Python creates a pattern object that can be reused in multiple locations—much as a compiled program can be executed multiple times. Now, you call the function match() on our compiled pattern and the text to be searched. This leads to the following result:

```
## Result
print(pattern.match(text_1))
# <re.Match object; span=(0, 34), match='crypto-bot that is trading Bitcoin'>

print(pattern.match(text_2))
# None
```

The string variable text_1 matches the pattern (indicated by the resulting match object), but text_2 doesn't (indicated by the result None). Although the textual representation of the first matching object doesn't look pretty, it gives a clear hint that the given string 'crypto-bot that is trading Bitcoin' matches the regular expression.

Analyzing Hyperlinks of HTML Documents

In the preceding section, you learned how to search a string for a large number of patterns by using the regex pattern .{x,y}. This section goes further, introducing many more regular expressions.

The Basics

Knowing more regular expressions will help you solve real-world problems quickly and concisely. So what are the most important regular expressions? Study the following list carefully because we'll use all of them in this chapter. Just view the ones you've already seen as a small repetition exercise.

- The dot regex . matches an arbitrary character.

- The asterisk regex *<pattern>** matches an arbitrary number of the regex *<pattern>*. Note that this includes zero matching instances.

- The at-least-one regex *<pattern>*+ can match an arbitrary number of *<pattern>* but must match at least one instance.

- The zero-or-one regex *<pattern>*? matches either zero or one instances of *<pattern>*.

- The nongreedy asterisk regex *? matches as few arbitrary characters as possible to match the overall regex.

- The regex *<pattern>*{m} matches exactly m copies of *<pattern>*.

- The regex *<pattern>*{m,n} matches between m and n copies of *<pattern>*.

- The regex *<pattern_1>*|*<pattern_2>* matches either *<pattern_1>* or *<pattern_2>*.

- The regex *<pattern_1><pattern_2>* matches *<pattern_1>* and then *<pattern_2>*.

- The regex (*<pattern>*) matches *<pattern>*. The parentheses group regular expressions so you can control the order of execution (for example, (*<pattern_1><pattern_2>*)|*<pattern_3>* is different from *<pattern_1>* (*<pattern_2>*|*<pattern_3>*). The parentheses regex also creates a matching group, as you'll see later in the section.

Let's consider a short example. Say you create the regex b?(.a)*. Which patterns will the regex match? The regex matches all patterns starting with zero or one b and an arbitrary number of two-character-sequences ending in the character 'a'. Hence, the strings 'bcacaca', 'cadaea', '' (the empty string), and 'aaaaaa' would all match the regex.

Before diving into the next one-liner, let's quickly discuss when to use which *regex function*. The three most important regex functions are re.match(), re.search(), and re.findall(). You've already seen two of them, but let's study them more thoroughly in this example:

```
import re

text = '''
"One can never have enough socks", said Dumbledore.
"Another Christmas has come and gone and I didn't
get a single pair. People will insist on giving me books."
Christmas Quote
'''

regex = 'Christ.*'

print(re.match(regex, text))
# None

print(re.search(regex, text))
# <re.Match object; span=(62, 102), match="Christmas has come and gone and I didn't">

print(re.findall(regex, text))
# ["Christmas has come and gone and I didn't", 'Christmas Quote']
```

All three functions take the regex and the string to be searched as an input. The match() and search() functions return a match object (or None if the regex did not match anything). The match object stores the position of the match and more advanced meta-information. The function match() does not find the regex in the string (it returns None). Why? Because the function looks for the pattern only *at the beginning* of the string. The function search() searches for the first occurrence of the regex *anywhere* in the string. Therefore, it finds the match "Christmas has come and gone and I didn't".

The findall() function has the most intuitive output, but it's also the least useful for further processing. The result of findall() is a sequence of strings rather than a match object—so it doesn't give us information about the precise location of the match. That said, findall() has its uses: in contrast to the match() and search() methods, the function findall() retrieves *all* matched patterns, which is useful when you want to quantify how often a word appears in a text (for example, the string 'Juliet' in the text 'Romeo and Juliet' or the string 'crypto' in an article about cryptocurrency).

The Code

Say your company asks you to create a small web bot that crawls web pages and checks whether they contain links to the domain *finxter.com*. They also ask you to make sure the hyperlink descriptions contain the strings 'test' or 'puzzle'. In HTML, hyperlinks are enclosed in an <a></a> tag environment. The hyperlink itself is defined as the value of the href attribute. So more precisely, the goal is to solve the following problem, depicted in Listing 5-3: given a string, find all hyperlinks that point to the domain *finxter.com* and contain the strings 'test' or 'puzzle' in the link description.

```
## Dependencies
import re


## Data
page = '''
<!DOCTYPE html>
<html>
<body>

<h1>My Programming Links</h1>
<a href="https://app.finxter.com/">test your Python skills</a>
<a href="https://blog.finxter.com/recursion/">Learn recursion</a>
<a href="https://nostarch.com/">Great books from NoStarchPress</a>
<a href="http://finxter.com/">Solve more Python puzzles</a>

</body>
</html>
'''


## One-Liner
practice_tests = re.findall("(<a.*?finxter.*?(test|puzzle).*?>)", page)


## Result
print(practice_tests)
```

Listing 5-3: One-liner solution to analyze web page links

This code finds two occurrences of the regular expression. Which ones?

How It Works

The data consists of a simple HTML web page (stored as a multiline string) containing a list of hyperlinks (the tag environment `<a href="">`*link text*`</a>`). The one-liner solution uses the function `re.findall()` to check the regular expression (`<a.*?finxter.*?(test|puzzle).*?>`). This way, the regular expression returns all occurrences in the tag environment `<a. . .>` with the following restrictions.

After the opening tag, you match an arbitrary number of characters (nongreedily, to prevent the regex from "chewing up" multiple HTML tag environments), followed by the string `'finxter'`. Next, you match an arbitrary number of characters (nongreedily), followed by one occurrence of either the string `'test'` or the string `'puzzle'`. Again, you match an arbitrary number of characters (nongreedily), followed by the closing tag. This way, you find all hyperlink tags that contain the respective strings. Note that this regex also matches tags where the strings `'test'` or `'puzzle'` occur within the link itself. Please also note that you use only nongreedy asterisk operators `'.*?'` to ensure that you always search for minimal matches rather than matching—for example, a very long string enclosed in multiple nested tag environments.

The result of the one-liner is the following:

```
## Result
print(practice_tests)
# [('<a href="https://app.finxter.com/">test your Python skills</a>', 'test'),
#  ('<a href="http://finxter.com/">Solve more Python puzzles</a>', 'puzzle')]
```

Two hyperlinks match our regular expression: the result of the one-liner is a list with two elements. However, each element is a tuple of strings rather than a simple string. This is different from the results of `findall()`, which we've discussed in previous code snippets. What's the reason for this behavior? The return type is a list of tuples—with one tuple value for each *matching group* enclosed in (). For instance, the regex (`test|puzzle`) uses the parentheses notation to create a matching group. If you use matching groups in your regex, the function `re.findall()` will add one tuple value for every matched group. The tuple value is the substring that matches this particular group. For example, in our case, the substring `'puzzle'` matches the group (`test|puzzle`). Let's dive more deeply into the topic of matching groups to clarify this concept.

Extracting Dollars from a String

This one-liner shows you another practical application of regular expressions. Here, you're working as a financial analyst. As your company considers acquiring another company, you're assigned to read the other company's reports. You're particularly interested in all dollar figures. Now, you could scan the whole document manually, but the work is tedious, and you don't want to spend your best hours of the day doing tedious work. So you decide to write a small Python script. But what's the best way of doing it?

The Basics

Fortunately, you've read this regex tutorial, so instead of wasting a lot of time writing your own lengthy, error-prone Python parser, you go for the clean solution with regular expressions—a wise choice. But before you dive into the problem, let's discuss three more regex concepts.

First, sooner or later you want to match a special character that's also used as a special character by the regex language. In this case, you need to use the prefix \ to *escape* the meaning of the special character. For example, to match the parenthesis character '(', which is normally used for regex groups, you need to escape it with the regex \(. This way, the regex character '(' loses its special meaning.

Second, the square bracket environment [ ] allows you to define a range of specific characters to be matched. For example, the regex [0-9] matches one of the following characters: '0', '1', '2', ..., '9'. Another example is the regex [a-e], which matches one of the following characters: 'a', 'b', 'c', 'd', 'e'.

Third, as we discussed in the previous one-liner section, the parentheses regex (*pattern*) indicates a *group*. Every regex can have one or multiple groups. When using the re.findall() function on a regex with groups, only the matched groups are returned as a tuple of strings—one for each group—rather than the whole matched string. For example, the regex hello(world) called on the string 'helloworld' would match the whole string but return only the matched group world. On the other hand, when using two nested groups in the regex (hello(world)), the result of the re.findall() function would be a tuple of all matched groups ('helloworld', 'world'). Study the following code to understand nested groups completely:

```
string = 'helloworld'

regex_1 = 'hello(world)'
regex_2 = '(hello(world))'

res_1 = re.findall(regex_1, string)
res_2 = re.findall(regex_2, string)

print(res_1)
# ['world']
print(res_2)
# [('helloworld', 'world')]
```

Now, you know everything you need to know to understand the following code snippet.

The Code

To recap, you want to investigate all monetary numbers from a given company report. Specifically, your goal is to solve the following problem: given a string, find a list of all occurrences of dollar amounts with optional decimal values. The following example strings are valid matches: $10, $10., or $10.00021. How can you achieve this efficiently in a single line of code? Take a look at Listing 5-4.

```
## Dependencies
import re


## Data
report = '''
If you invested $1 in the year 1801, you would have $18087791.41 today.
This is a 7.967% return on investment.
But if you invested only $0.25 in 1801, you would end up with $4521947.8525.
'''


## One-Liner
dollars = [x[0] for x in re.findall('(\$[0-9]+(\.[0-9]*)?)', report)]


## Result
print(dollars)
```

Listing 5-4: One-liner solution to find all dollar amounts in a text

Take a guess: what's the output of this code snippet?

How It Works

The report contains four dollar values in various formats. The goal is to develop a regex that matches all of them. You design the regex (\$[0-9]+ (.[0-9]*)?) that matches the following patterns. First, it matches the dollar sign $ (you escape it because it's a special regex character). Second, it matches a number with an arbitrary number of digits between 0 and 9 (but at least one digit). Third, it matches an arbitrary number of decimal values after the (escaped) dot character '.' (this last match is optional as indicated by the zero-or-one regex ?).

On top of that, you use list comprehension to extract only the first tuple value of all three resulting matches. Again, the default result of the re.findall() function is a list of tuples, with one tuple for each successful match and one tuple value for each group within the match:

```
[('$1', ''), ('$18087791.41', '.41'), ('$0.25', '.25'), ('$4521947.8525', '.8525')]
```

You're interested in only the global group—the first value in the tuple. You filter out the other values by using list comprehension and get the following result:

```
## Result
print(dollars)
# ['$1 ', '$18087791.41', '$0.25', '$4521947.8525']
```

It's worth noting again that implementing even a simple parser without the powerful capabilities of regular expressions would be difficult and error-prone!

Finding Nonsecure HTTP URLs

This one-liner shows you how to solve one of those small, time-intensive problems that web developers often run into. Say you own a programming blog and you've just moved your website from the unsecure protocol http to the (more) secure protocol https. However, your old articles still point to the old URLs. How can you find all occurrences of the old URLs?

The Basics

In the preceding section, you learned how to use square bracket notation to specify an arbitrary range of characters. For example, the regular expression [0-9] matches a single-digit number with a value from 0 to 9. However, the square bracket notation is more powerful than that. You can use an arbitrary combination of characters within the square brackets to specify exactly which characters match—and which don't. For example, the regular expression [0-3a-c]+ matches the strings '01110' and '01c22a' but not the strings '443' and '00cd'. You can also specify a fixed set of characters *not* to match by using the symbol ^: the regular expression [^0-3a-c]+ matches the strings '4444d' and 'Python' but not the strings '001' and '01c22a'.

The Code

Here our input is a (multiline) string, and our aim is to find all occurrences of valid URLs that start with the prefix *http://*. However, don't consider invalid URLs without a top-level domain (there has to be at least one . in the found URL). Take a look at Listing 5-5.

```
## Dependencies
import re


## Data
article = '''
The algorithm has important practical applications
http://blog.finxter.com/applications/
in many basic data structures such as sets, trees,
dictionaries, bags, bag trees, bag dictionaries,
hash sets, https://blog.finxter.com/sets-in-python/
hash tables, maps, and arrays. http://blog.finxter.com/
http://not-a-valid-url
http:/bla.ba.com
http://bo.bo.bo.bo.bo.bo/
http://bo.bo.bo.bo.bo.bo/333483--33343-/
'''
```

```
## One-Liner
stale_links = re.findall('http://[a-z0-9_\-.]+\.[a-z0-9_\-/]+', article)


## Results
print(stale_links)
```

Listing 5-5: One-liner solution to find valid http:// *URLs*

Again, try to come up with the output the code will produce before looking up the correct output that follows.

How It Works

In the regular expression, you analyze a given multiline string (potentially an old blog article) to find all URLs that start with the string prefix http://. The regular expression expects a positive number of (lowercase) characters, numbers, underscores, hyphens, or dots ([a-z0-9_\-.]+). Note that you need to escape the hyphen (\-) because it normally indicates a range within the square brackets. Similarly, you need to escape the dot (\.) because you actually want to match the dot and not an arbitrary character. This results in the following output:

```
## Results
print(stale_links)
# ['http://blog.finxter.com/applications/',
#  'http://blog.finxter.com/',
#  'http://bo.bo.bo.bo.bo.bo/',
#  'http://bo.bo.bo.bo.bo.bo/333483--33343-/']
```

Four valid URLs may need to be moved to the more secure HTTPS protocol.

At this point, you've already mastered the most important features of regular expressions. But there's a level of deep understanding that you'll reach only by practicing and studying a lot of examples—and regular expressions are no exception. Let's study a few more practical examples of how regular expressions can make your life easier.

Validating the Time Format of User Input, Part 1

Let's learn to check the correctness of user-input formatting. Say you write a web application that calculates health statistics based on the sleep duration of your users. Your users enter the time they went to bed and the time they wake up. An example for a correct time format is 12:45, but because web bots are spamming your user input fields, a lot of "dirty" data is causing unnecessary processing overhead on your servers. To address this issue, you write a time-format checker that determines whether the input is worth processing further with your backend application. With regular expressions, writing the code takes only a few minutes.

The Basics

In the previous few sections, you've learned about the re.search(), re.match(), and re.findall() functions. These are not the only regex functions. In this section, you'll use re.fullmatch(*regex, string*), which checks whether the regex matches the *full* string as the name suggests.

Furthermore, you'll use the regex syntax *pattern{m,n}* that matches between *m* and *n* instances of the regex *pattern*, but no more and no less. Note that it attempts to match the maximal number of occurrences of *pattern*. Here's an example:

```
import re

print(re.findall('x{3,5}y', 'xy'))
# []
print(re.findall('x{3,5}y', 'xxxy'))
# ['xxxy']
print(re.findall('x{3,5}y', 'xxxxxy'))
# ['xxxxxy']
print(re.findall('x{3,5}y', 'xxxxxxy'))
# ['xxxxxy']
```

Using the bracket notation, the code doesn't match substrings with fewer than three and more than five 'x' characters.

The Code

Our goal is to write a function input_ok that takes a string argument and checks whether it has the (time) format *XX:XX*, where *X* is a number from 0 to 9; see Listing 5-6. Note that, for now, you accept semantically wrong time formats such as 12:86, but the next one-liner section tackles this more advanced problem.

```
## Dependencies
import re


## Data
inputs = ['18:29', '23:55', '123', 'ab:de', '18:299', '99:99']


## One-Liner
input_ok = lambda x: re.fullmatch('[0-9]{2}:[0-9]{2}', x) != None


## Result
for x in inputs:
    print(input_ok(x))
```

Listing 5-6: One-liner solution to check whether a given user input matches the general time format XX:XX

Before you move on, try to determine the results of the six function calls in this code.

How It Works

The data consists of six input strings as received by the frontend of your web application. Are they correctly formatted? To check this, you create the function input_ok by using a lambda expression with one input argument x and a Boolean output. You use the function fullmatch(*regex*, x) and attempt to match the input argument x by using our time-formatting regex. If you couldn't match it, the result takes the value None and the Boolean output becomes False. Otherwise, the Boolean output is True.

The regex is simple: [0-9]{2}:[0-9]{2}. This pattern matches two leading numbers from 0 to 9, followed by the colon:, followed by two trailing numbers from 0 to 9. Thus, the result of Listing 5-6 is the following:

```
## Result
for x in inputs:
    print(input_ok(x))

'''
True
True
False
False
False
True
'''
```

The function input_ok correctly identifies the correct formats of the time inputs. In this one-liner, you've learned how highly practical tasks—that would otherwise take multiple lines of code and more effort—can be finished successfully in a few seconds with the right tool set.

Validating Time Format of User Input, Part 2

In this section, you'll dive deeper into validating the time format of user inputs to solve the problem of the previous section: invalid time inputs such as 99:99 should not be considered valid matches.

The Basics

A useful strategy to solve problems is to address them hierarchically. First, strip down the problem to its core and solve the easier variant. Then, refine the solution to match your specific (and more complicated) problem. This section refines the previous solution in an important way: it doesn't allow invalid time inputs such as 99:99 or 28:66. Hence, the problem is more specific (and more complicated), but you can reuse parts of our old solution.

The Code

Our goal is to write a function `input_ok` that takes a string argument and checks whether it has the (time) format *XX:XX*, where *X* is a number between 0 and 9; see Listing 5-7. Additionally, the given time must be a valid time format in the 24-hour time ranging from 00:00 to 23:59.

```
## Dependencies
import re


## Data
inputs = ['18:29', '23:55', '123', 'ab:de', '18:299', '99:99']


## One-Liner
input_ok = lambda x: re.fullmatch('([01][0-9]|2[0-3]):[0-5][0-9]', x) != None

## Result
for x in inputs:
    print(input_ok(x))
```

Listing 5-7: One-liner solution to check whether a given user input matches the general time format `XX:XX` and is valid in the 24-hour time

This code prints six lines. What are they?

How It Works

As mentioned in the introduction of this section, you can reuse the solution of the previous one-liner to solve this problem easily. The code stays the same—you modified only the regular expression `([01][0-9]|2[0-3]):[0-5][0-9]`. The first part `([01][0-9]|2[0-3])` is a group that matches all possible hours of the day. You use the or operator `|` to differentiate hours 00 to 19 on the one hand, and hours 20 to 23 on the other hand. The second part `[0-5][0-9]` matches the minutes of the day from 00 to 59. The result is, therefore, as follows:

```
## Result
for x in inputs:
    print(input_ok(x))

'''
True
True
False
False
False
False
'''
```

Note that the sixth line of the output indicates that the time `99:99` is no longer considered a valid user input. This one-liner shows how to use regular expressions to check whether the user input matches the semantic requirements of your application.

Duplicate Detection in Strings

This one-liner introduces an exciting capability of regular expressions: reusing parts you've already matched later in the same regex. This powerful extension allows you to solve a new set of problems, including detecting strings with duplicated characters.

The Basics

This time, you're working as a computer linguistics researcher analyzing how certain word usages change over time. You use published books to classify and track word usage. Your professor asks you to analyze whether there's a trend toward a more frequent use of duplicate characters in words. For example, the word 'hello' contains the duplicate character 'l', while the word 'spoon' contains the duplicate character 'o'. However, the word 'mama' would not be counted as a word with a duplicate character 'a'.

The naive solution to this problem is to enumerate all possible duplicate characters 'aa', 'bb', 'cc', 'dd', . . . , 'zz' and combine them in an either-or regex. This solution is tedious and not easily generalized. What if your professor changes their mind and asks you to check for repeat characters with up to one character in between (for example, the string 'mama' would now be a match)?

No problem: there's a simple, clean, and effective solution if you know the regex feature of named groups. You've already learned about groups that are enclosed in parentheses (...). As the name suggests, a *named group* is just a group with a name. For instance, you can define a named group around the pattern ... with the name name by using the syntax (?P<name>...). After you define a named group, you can use it anywhere in your regular expression with the syntax (?P=name). Consider the following example:

```
import re

pattern = '(?P<quote>[\'"]).*(?P=quote)'
text = 'She said "hi"'
print(re.search(pattern, text))
# <re.Match object; span=(9, 13), match='"hi"'>
```

In the code, you search for substrings that are enclosed in either single or double quotes. To accomplish that, you first match the opening quote by using the regex ['"] (you escape the single quote, \', to avoid Python wrongly assuming that the single quote indicates the end of the string). Then, you use the same group to match the closing quote of the same character (either a single or double quote).

Before diving into the code, note that you can match arbitrary whitespaces with the regex \s. Also, you can match characters that are *not* in a set Y by using the syntax [^Y]. That's everything you need to know to solve our problem.

The Code

Consider the problem illustrated in Listing 5-8: given a text, find all words that contain duplicate characters. A *word* in this case is defined as any series of non-whitespace characters separated by an arbitrary number of whitespace characters.

```
## Dependencies
import re


## Data
text = '''
It was a bright cold day in April, and the clocks were
striking thirteen. Winston Smith, his chin nuzzled into
his breast in an effort to escape the vile wind, slipped
quickly through the glass doors of Victory Mansions,
though not quickly enough to prevent a swirl of gritty
dust from entering along with him.
-- George Orwell, 1984
'''


## One-Liner
duplicates = re.findall('([^\s]*(?P<x>[^\s])(?P=x)[^\s]*)', text)


## Results
print(duplicates)
```

Listing 5-8: One-liner solution to find all duplicate characters

What are the words with duplicate characters found in this code?

How It Works

The regex (?P<x>[^\s]) defines a new group with the name x. The group consists of only a single arbitrary character that is not the whitespace character. The regex (?P=x) immediately follows the named group x. It simply matches the same character matched by the group x. You've found the duplicate characters! However, the goal is not to find duplicate characters, but words with duplicate characters. So you match an arbitrary number of non-whitespace characters [^\s]* before and after the duplicate characters.

The output of Listing 5-8 is the following:

```
## Results
print(duplicates)
'''
[('thirteen.', 'e'), ('nuzzled', 'z'), ('effort', 'f'),
('slipped', 'p'), ('glass', 's'), ('doors', 'o'),
('gritty', 't'), ('--', '-'), ('Orwell,', 'l')]
'''
```

The regex finds all words with duplicate characters in the text. Note that there are two groups in the regex of Listing 5-8, so every element returned by the re.findall() function consists of a tuple of matched groups. You've already seen this behavior in previous sections.

In this section, you've enhanced your regex tool set with one powerful tool: named groups. In combination with two minor regex features of matching arbitrary whitespace characters with \s and defining a set of characters that are not matched with the operator [^...], you've made serious progress toward Python regex proficiency.

Detecting Word Repetitions

In the preceding section, you learned about named groups. The goal of this section is to show you more advanced ways of using this powerful feature.

The Basics

While working as a researcher over the last few years, I spent most of my time writing, reading, and editing research papers. When editing my research papers, a colleague used to complain that I was using the same words repeatedly (and too closely in the text). Wouldn't it be useful to have a tool that checks your writing programmatically?

The Code

You're given a string consisting of lowercase, whitespace-separated words, without special characters. Find a matching substring where the first and the last word are the same (repetition) and in-between are at most 10 words. See Listing 5-9.

```
## Dependencies
import re


## Data
text = 'if you use words too often words become used'


## One-Liner
style_problems = re.search('\s(?P<x>[a-z]+)\s+([a-z]+\s+){0,10}(?P=x)\s', ' ' + text + ' ')


## Results
print(style_problems)
```

Listing 5-9: One-liner solution to find word repetitions

Does this code find word repetitions?

How It Works

Again, you assume that a given text consists of only whitespace-separated, lowercase words. Now, you search the text by using a regular expression. It might look complex at first, but let's break it down piece by piece:

```
'❶\s(?P<x>[a-z]+)\s+❷([a-z]+\s+){0,10}❸(?P=x)\s'
```

You start with a single whitespace character. This is important to ensure that you start with a whole word (and not with a suffix of a word). Then, you match a named group x that consists of a positive number of lowercase characters from 'a' to 'z', followed by a positive number of whitespaces ❶.

You proceed with 0 to 10 words, where each word consists of a positive number of lowercase characters from 'a' to 'z', followed by a positive number of whitespaces ❷.

You finish with the named group x, followed by a whitespace character to ensure that the last match is a whole word (and not only a prefix of a word) ❸.

The following is the output of the code snippet:

```
## Results
print(style_problems)
# <re.Match object; span=(12, 35), match=' words too often words '>
```

You found a matching substring that may (or may not) be considered as bad style.

In this one-liner, you stripped down the problem of finding duplicate words to its core and solved this easier variant. Note that in practice, you'd have to include more complicated cases such as special characters, a mix of lowercase and uppercase characters, numbers, and so on. Alternatively, you could do some preprocessing to bring the text into the desired form of lowercase, whitespace-separated words, without special characters.

EXERCISE 5-1

Write a Python script that allows for more special characters, such as characters to structure your sentences (period, colon, comma).

Modifying Regex Patterns in a Multiline String

In the final regex one-liner, you'll learn how to modify a text rather than matching only parts of it.

The Basics

To replace all occurrences of a certain regex pattern with a new string replacement in a given text, use the regex function re.sub(regex, replacement, text). This way, you can quickly edit large text bases without a lot of manual labor.

In the previous sections, you learned how to match patterns that occur in the text. But what if you don't want to match a certain pattern if another pattern occurs? The *negative lookahead* regex pattern A(?!X) matches a regex A if the regex X does not match afterward. For example, the regex not (?!good) would match the string 'this is not great' but would not match the string 'this is not good'.

The Code

Our data is a string, and our task is to replace all occurrences of Alice Wonderland with 'Alice Doe', but not to replace occurrences of 'Alice Wonderland' (enclosed in single quotes). See Listing 5-10.

```
## Dependencies
import re


## Data
text = '''
Alice Wonderland married John Doe.
The new name of former 'Alice Wonderland' is Alice Doe.
Alice Wonderland replaces her old name 'Wonderland' with her new name 'Doe'.
Alice's sister Jane Wonderland still keeps her old name.
'''


## One-Liner
updated_text = re.sub("Alice Wonderland(?!')", 'Alice Doe', text)


## Result
print(updated_text)
```

Listing 5-10: One-liner solution to replace patterns in a text

This code prints the updated text. What is it?

How It Works

You replace all occurrences of Alice Wonderland with Alice Doe, but not the ones that end with the single quote '. You do this by using a negative lookahead. Note that you check only whether the closing quote exists. For example, a string *with* an opening quote but *without* a closing quote would match, and you'd simply replace it. This may not be desired in general, but it leads to the desired behavior in our example string:

```
## Result
print(updated_text)
'''
Alice Doe married John Doe.
The new name of former 'Alice Wonderland' is Alice Doe.
Alice Doe replaces her old name 'Wonderland' with her new name 'Doe'.
Alice's sister Jane Wonderland still keeps her old name.
'''
```

You can see that the original name of 'Alice Wonderland' is left unchanged when enclosed in single quotes—which was the goal of this code snippet.

Summary

This chapter covered a lot of ground. You've learned about regular expressions, which you can use to match patterns in a given string. In particular, you've learned about the functions re.compile(), re.match(), re.search(), re.findall(), and re.sub(). Together, they cover a high percentage of regular expression use cases. You can pick up other functions as you apply regular expressions in practice.

You've also learned about various basic regular expressions that you can combine (and recombine) in order to create more advanced regular expressions. You've learned about whitespaces, escaped characters, greedy/nongreedy operators, character sets (and negative characters sets), grouping and named groups, and negative lookaheads. And finally, you've learned that it's often better to solve a simplified variant of the original problem than trying to generalize too early.

The only thing left is to apply your new regex skill in practice. A good way of getting used to regular expressions is to start using them in your favorite text editor. Most advanced text and code editors (including Notepad++) ship with powerful regular expression functionality. Also, consider regular expressions when working with textual data (for example when writing emails, blog articles, books, and code). Regular expressions will make your life easier and save you many hours of tedious work.

In the next chapter, we'll dive into the supreme discipline of coding: algorithms.

6

ALGORITHMS

Algorithms are ancient concepts. An *algorithm* is nothing more than a set of instructions, much like a cooking recipe. However, the *role* algorithms play in society is increasing drastically in importance: algorithms and algorithmic decision-making are ubiquitous as computers become a larger and larger part of our lives.

A 2018 study highlights that "Data, in the form of observations about our world, permeate modern society. . . . This information can in turn be used to make informed—and in some cases even fully automated—decisions. . . . It seems likely that such algorithms will interface with human decision-making, a development necessary to gain societal acceptance and thus wide-scale use."

NOTE *For more information on this study, see "The Growing Ubiquity of Algorithms in Society: Implications, Impacts, and Innovations" by S. C. Olhede and P. J. Wolfe at* https://royalsocietypublishing.org/doi/full/10.1098/rsta.2017 .0364#d2696064e1.

As society undergoes major trends in automation, artificial intelligence, and ubiquitous computing, the societal gap between those who understand algorithms and those who don't grows rapidly. For example, the logistics sector undergoes a major trend toward automation—with self-driving cars and trucks on the rise—and professional drivers face the fact that algorithms take over their jobs.

The constantly shifting landscape of sought-after skills and jobs in the 21st century makes it imperative for young people to understand, control, and manipulate basic algorithms. While the only constant is change, the concepts and basics of algorithms and algorithmic theory form the basis upon which much of the upcoming changes are built. Roughly speaking, understand algorithms and you'll be well equipped to thrive in the upcoming decades.

This chapter aims to improve your understanding of algorithms, focusing more on your intuition and a well-rounded understanding of concepts and practical implementations than on theory. While algorithmic theory is as important as practical implementations and conceptual understanding, many great books focus on the theory part. After reading this chapter, you will intuitively understand some of the most popular algorithms in computer science—and improve your practical Python implementation skills. This may provide you a strong foundation for the upcoming technological breakthroughs.

NOTE   *The book* Introduction to Algorithms *by Thomas Cormen et al. (MIT Press, 2009) is an excellent follow-up resource on algorithmic theory.*

Let's start with a small algorithm to solve a simple problem that is relevant for programmers who want to find good jobs.

Finding Anagrams with Lambda Functions and Sorting

Anagrams are a popular topic in programming interviews to test your computer science vocabulary and how good you are at developing your own simple algorithms. In this section, you'll learn about a simple algorithm to find anagrams in Python.

The Basics

Two words are *anagrams* if they consist of the same characters and if every character of the first word appears in the second word exactly once. This is illustrated in Figure 6-1 and in the following examples:

- "listen" → "silent"
- "funeral " → "real fun"
- "elvis" → "lives"

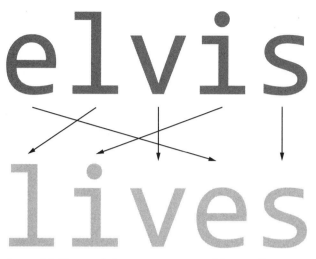

Figure 6-1: The word elvis is an anagram of the word lives.

We'll now work on this problem and arrive at a concise Pythonic solution to figuring out whether two words are anagrams. Let's start coding.

The Code

Our goal is to write a function is_anagram() that takes two strings x1 and x2 and returns True if those are anagrams! Before you read on, pause for a moment and think about the problem. How would you approach it in Python? Listing 6-1 shows one solution.

```
## One-Liner
❶ is_anagram = lambda x1, x2: sorted(x1) == sorted(x2)


## Results
print(is_anagram("elvis", "lives"))
print(is_anagram("elvise", "livees"))
print(is_anagram("elvis", "dead"))
```

Listing 6-1: One-liner solution to check whether two strings are anagrams

This code prints three lines. What are they?

How It Works

Two strings are anagrams if they have the same sorted character sequence, so our method is to sort both strings and then make an element-wise comparison. It's that easy. There is no need for external dependencies. You simply create a function is_anagram() ❶ by using the lambda function definition (see Chapter 1) with two arguments x1 and x2. The function returns the result of the expression sorted(x1) == sorted(x2), which is True if the sorted character sequences consist of the same characters. Here's the output of the two sorted character sequences:

```
print(sorted("elvis"))
# ['e', 'i', 'l', 's', 'v']

print(sorted("lives"))
# ['e', 'i', 'l', 's', 'v']
```

Both strings 'elvis' and 'lives' consist of the same characters, so the sorted list representation is the same. The result of the three print statements is the following:

```
## Results
print(is_anagram("elvis", "lives")) # True
print(is_anagram("elvise", "livees")) # True
print(is_anagram("elvis", "dead")) # False
```

As a small side note for advanced coders: the runtime complexity of sorting a sequence of n elements in Python grows asymptotically like the function $n \ log(n)$. That means our one-liner algorithm is more efficient than the naive solution of checking whether every character exists in both strings and removing the character if this is the case. The naive algorithm grows asymptotically like the quadratic function $n**2$.

However, there's another efficient way, called *histogramming*, whereby you create a histogram for both strings that counts the number of occurrences of all characters in that string, and then compare the two histograms. Assuming a constant-sized alphabet, the runtime complexity of histogramming is linear; it grows asymptotically like the function n. Feel free to implement this algorithm as a small exercise!

Finding Palindromes with Lambda Functions and Negative Slicing

This section introduces another computer science term that's popular in interview questions: palindromes. You'll use a one-liner to check whether two words are palindromes of each other.

The Basics

First things first: what is a palindrome? A *palindrome* can be defined as a sequence of elements (for example, a string or a list) that reads the same backward as it does forward. Here are a few fun examples that are palindromes if you take out the whitespace:

- "Mr Owl ate my metal worm"
- "Was it a car or a cat I saw?"
- "Go hang a salami, I'm a lasagna hog"

- "Rats live on no evil star"
- "Hannah"
- "Anna"
- "Bob"

Our one-liner solution will require your basic understanding of slicing. As you know from Chapter 2, slicing is a Python-specific concept for carving out a range of values from sequence types such as lists or strings. Slicing uses the concise notation [start:stop:step] to slice a sequence starting at index start (inclusive) and ending at index stop (exclusive). The third parameter step allows you to define the *step size*, which is how many characters from the original sequence your slice will skip before taking the next character (for example, step=2 means that your slice will consist of only every other character). When using a negative step size, the string is traversed in reverse order.

This is everything you need to know to come up with a short and concise one-liner solution in Python.

The Code

When given a string, you want your code to check whether the reverse sequence of characters equals the original sequence, to determine whether the string is a palindrome. Listing 6-2 shows the solution.

```
## One-Liner
is_palindrome = lambda phrase: phrase == phrase[::-1]


## Result
print(is_palindrome("anna"))
print(is_palindrome("kdljfasjf"))
print(is_palindrome("rats live on no evil star"))
```

Listing 6-2: One-liner solution to check whether a phrase is a palindrome

How It Works

The simple one-liner solution does not depend on any external library. You define a lambda function that takes a single argument phrase—the string to be tested—and returns a Boolean value that says whether the sequence of characters remains unchanged when reversed. To reverse the string, you use slicing (see Chapter 2).

The result of the one-liner code snippet is the following:

```
## Result
print(is_palindrome("anna")) # True
print(is_palindrome("kdljfasjf")) # False
print(is_palindrome("rats live on no evil star")) # True
```

The first and third strings are palindromes, but the second isn't. Next let's dive into another popular computer science concept: permutations.

Counting Permutations with Recursive Factorial Functions

This section explains a simple and effective way of computing the factorial in a single line of code to figure out the maximum number of possible permutations in a data set.

The Basics

Consider the following problem: England's Premier League has 20 soccer teams, each of which can reach any of the 20 ranks at the end of the season. Given 20 fixed teams, you can calculate how many possible versions of these rankings exist. Note that the question is not how many rankings a single team can achieve (the answer would be 20) but how many total rankings of all teams exist. Figure 6-2 shows just three possible rankings.

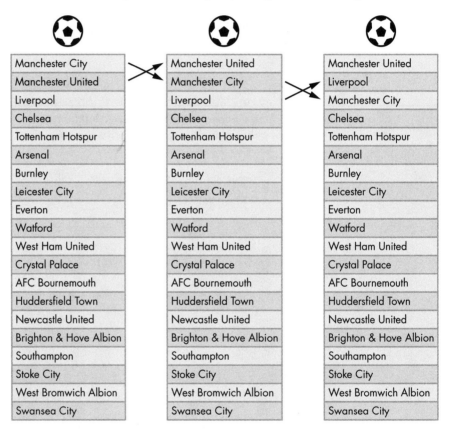

Figure 6-2: Three possible rankings of the soccer teams in England's Premier League

In computer science terminology, you would denote each ranking as a *permutation*, defined as a specific order of set elements. Our goal is to find the number of possible permutations of a given set. The number of those permutations has important implications for programs involved in betting applications, match prediction, and game analysis. For example, if each of 100 different rankings has the same initial probability, the probability of a specific ranking is 1/100 = 1 percent. This can be used as a base probability (*a priori probability*) for game-prediction algorithms. Under these assumptions, a randomly guessed ranking has a 1 percent probability of being the correct outcome after one season.

To calculate the number of permutations of a given set of n elements, you can use the factorial function $n!$. In the next few paragraphs, you'll learn why this is the case. The factorial is defined as follows:

$$n! = n \times (n-1) \times (n-2) \times \ldots \times 1$$

For example:

$$1! = 1$$
$$3! = 3 \times 2 \times 1 = 6$$
$$10! = 10 \times 9 \times 8 \times 7 \times 6 \times 5 \times 4 \times 3 \times 2 \times 1 = 3{,}628{,}800$$
$$20! = 20 \times 19 \times 18 \times \ldots \times 3 \times 2 \times 1 = 2{,}432{,}902{,}008{,}176{,}640{,}000$$

Let's take a look at how this works. Say you have a set of 10 elements $S = \{s0, s1, s2, \ldots, s9\}$ and 10 buckets $B = \{b0, b1, b2, \ldots, b9\}$. You want to place exactly one element from S into each bucket. In the soccer example, the 20 teams are the elements, and the 20 table ranks are the buckets. To get one specific permutation of S, you simply place all elements into all buckets. The number of different ways of assigning elements to buckets is the total number of permutations of elements in S.

The following algorithm determines the number of permutations for a set with 10 elements (which need to be placed into 10 buckets):

1. Take the first element from the set S. There are *10 empty buckets* so you have *10 options* for where you can place the element. You place one element in a bucket.

2. Now one bucket is occupied. Take the second element from the set. There now remain *9 empty buckets* so you have *9 options*.

3. Finally, take the 10th (last) element from the set. Nine buckets are now occupied. There is only *one empty bucket*, so you have *one option*.

In total, you have $10 \times 9 \times 8 \times 7 \times 6 \times 5 \times 4 \times 3 \times 2 \times 1 = 10!$ options. Each potential placement of an element in a bucket represents one permutation of the set elements. The number of permutations of a set with n elements is therefore $n!$.

Recursively, the factorial function can also be defined as follows:

$$n! = n \times (n-1)!$$

The recursion base cases are defined as shown here:

$$1! = 0! = 1$$

The intuition behind these base cases is that a set with one element has one permutation, and a set with zero elements has one permutation (there is one way of assigning zero elements to zero buckets).

The Code

The one-liner in Listing 6-3 will compute the number of permutations *n!* of a set with *n* elements.

```
## The Data
n = 5


## The One-Liner
factorial = lambda n: n * factorial(n-1) if n > 1 else 1


## The Result
print(factorial(n))
```

Listing 6-3: One-liner solution defining the factorial function recursively

Try figuring out what the output of this code would be.

How It Works

In the code, you use the recursive definition of the factorial. Let's quickly improve our intuitive understanding of recursion. Stephen Hawking came up with a concise way to explain recursion: "To understand recursion, one must first understand recursion."

The Merriam-Webster dictionary defines recursion as "a computer programming technique involving the use of a . . . function . . . that calls itself one or more times until a specified condition is met, at which time the rest of each repetition is processed from the last one called to the first." At the heart of this definition is the *recursive function*, which is simply a function that calls itself. But if the function keeps calling itself, it would never stop.

For this reason, we set a certain base case. When the base case is met, the last function call terminates and returns a solution to the second-to-last function call. The second-to-last function call also returns the solution to the third-to-last function call. This causes a chain reaction of propagating the results to the higher recursion level until the first function call returns the final result. This may feel difficult to grasp in a few lines of English text, but stay with me: we will discuss this with the aid of the given one-liner example next.

In general, you create a recursive function *f* in four steps:

1. Break the original problem into smaller problem instances.
2. Take the smaller problem instances as the input of function *f* (which will then break the smaller input into even smaller problem instances and so on).
3. Define a *base case*, which is the smallest possible input that can be solved directly without any further call of the function *f*.
4. Specify how you can recombine the obtained smaller solutions into the larger solution.

You create a lambda function with one argument n and assign the lambda function to the name `factorial`. Finally, you call the named function `factorial(n-1)` to calculate the result of the function call `factorial(n)`. The value n could be the number of soccer teams in the Premier League (n=20) or any other value such as the one in Listing 6-3 (n=5).

Roughly speaking, you can use the simpler solution for `factorial(n-1)` to construct the solution of the harder problem `factorial(n)` by multiplying the former with the input argument n. As soon as you reach the recursion base case n <= 1, you simply return the hardcoded solution `factorial(1)` = `factorial(0)` = 1.

This algorithm shows how you can often find a simple, concise, and efficient way of solving problems by thoroughly understanding the problem first. Choosing the simplest solution idea is one of the most important things you can do when creating your own algorithms. Beginners often find they write cluttered and unnecessarily complicated code.

In this case, the recursive (one-liner) definition of the factorial is shorter than an iterative (one-liner) definition without recursion. As an exercise, try rewriting this one-liner without using a recursive definition and without external libraries—it's not trivial and certainly not that concise!

Finding the Levenshtein Distance

In this section, you'll learn about an important practical algorithm to calculate the Levenshtein distance. Understanding this algorithm is more complicated than previous algorithms, so you'll also train yourself to think through a problem clearly.

The Basics

The *Levenshtein distance* is a metric to calculate the distance between two strings; in other words, it's used to quantify the similarity of two strings. Its alternate name, the *edit distance*, describes precisely what it measures: the number of character edits (insertions, removals, or substitutions) needed to transform one string into another. The smaller the Levenshtein distance, the more similar the strings.

The Levenshtein distance has important applications in things like the autocorrection functionality on your smartphone. If you type *helo* in your WhatsApp messenger, your smartphone detects a word outside its library and selects several high-probability words as potential replacements, and then sorts them by Levenshtein distance. For example, the word with minimal Levenshtein distance and, hence, maximal similarity is the string 'hello', so your phone may automatically correct *helo* to *hello*.

Let's consider an example with the two less similar strings 'cat' and 'chello'. Knowing that the Levenshtein distance computes the minimal number of edits required to reach the second string starting from the first string, Table 6-1 shows the minimal sequence.

Table 6-1: The Minimal Sequence Needed to Change `'cat'` to `'chello'`

Current word	Edit made
cat	—
cht	Replace *a* with *h*
che	Replace *t* with *e*
chel	Insert *l* at position 3
chell	Insert *l* at position 4
chello	Insert *o* at position 5

Table 6-1 transforms the string `'cat'` to the string `'chello'` in five editing steps, meaning the Levenshtein distance is 5.

The Code

Now let's write a Python one-liner that calculates the Levenshtein distance of strings a and b, a and c, and b and c (see Listing 6-4).

```
## The Data
a = "cat"
b = "chello"
c = "chess"

## The One-Liner
ls = ❶lambda a, b: len(b) if not a else len(a) if not b else min(
  ❷ ls(a[1:], b[1:])+(a[0] != b[0]),
  ❸ ls(a[1:], b)+1,
  ❹ ls(a, b[1:])+1)

## The Result
print(ls(a,b))
print(ls(a,c))
print(ls(b,c))
```

Listing 6-4: Calculating the Levenshtein distance of two strings in one line

Based on what you know so far, try to calculate the output before running the program.

How It Works

Before diving into the code, let's quickly explore an important Python trick heavily used in this one-liner. In Python, *every* object has a truth value and is either True or False. Most objects are in fact True and, intuitively, you can probably guess the few objects that are False:

- The numerical value 0 is False.
- The empty string '' is False.
- The empty list [] is False.

- The empty set set() is False.
- The empty dictionary {} is False.

As a rule of thumb, Python objects are considered False if they are empty or zero. Equipped with this information, let's look at the first part of the Levenshtein function: you create a lambda function that takes two strings a and b and returns the number of edits required to transform string a into string b ❶.

There are two trivial cases: if string a is empty, the minimal edit distance is len(b), since you would just need to insert each character of string b. Similarly, if string b is empty, the minimal edit distance is len(a). That means if either string is empty, you can directly return the correct edit distance.

Let's say both strings are non-empty. You can simplify the problem by calculating the Levenshtein distance of smaller suffixes of the original strings a and b, as shown in Figure 6-3.

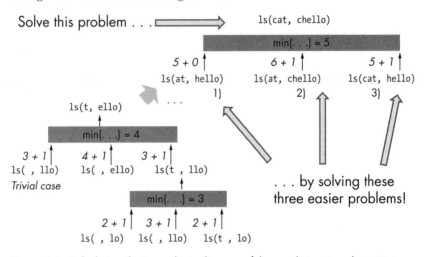

Figure 6-3: Calculating the Levenshtein distance of the words 'cat' and 'chello' recursively by solving the smaller problem instances first

To compute the Levenshtein distance between the strings 'cat' and 'chello' in a recursive manner, you solve the easier problems first (recursively):

1. You calculate the distance between the suffixes at and hello because if you know how to transform at into hello, you can easily transform cat into chello by modifying the first character (or by keeping the first character if both strings start with the same character). Assuming this distance is 5, you can now conclude that the distance between cat and chello is also at most 5 because you can reuse the exact same sequence of edits (both words begin with the character c and you don't have to edit this character).

2. You calculate the distance between at and chello. Assuming this distance is 6, you can now conclude that the distance between cat and

chello is at most 6 + 1 = 7 because you can simply remove the character c at the beginning of the first word (one additional operation). From there, you can reuse the exact same solution to come from at to chello.

3. You calculate the distance between cat and hello. Assuming this distance is 5, you can now conclude that the distance between cat and chello is at most 5 + 1 because you need to insert the character c at the beginning of the second word (one additional operation).

As these are all possible cases of what you can do with the first character (substitution, removal, insertion), the Levenshtein distance between cat and chello is the minimum of the three cases 1, 2, and 3. Let's now further examine the three cases in Listing 6-4.

First, you calculate the edit distance from a[1:] to b[1:] in a recursive manner ❷. If the leading characters a[0] and b[0] are different, you have to fix it by *replacing* a[0] by b[0], so you increment the edit distance by one. If the leading characters are the same, the solution of the simpler problem ls(a[1:], b[1:]) is also a solution to the more complex problem ls(a, b), as you've seen in Figure 6-3.

Second, you calculate the distance from a[1:] to b in a recursive manner ❸. Say you know the result of this distance (going from a[1:] to b)—how can you calculate the distance one step further from a to b? The answer is to simply *remove* the first character a[0] from the beginning of a, which is one additional operation. With this, you have reduced the more complicated problem to the easier one.

Third, you calculate the distance from a to b[1:] in a recursive manner ❹. Say you know the result of this distance (going from a to b[1:]). How can you calculate the distance from a to b? In this case, you can simply go one step further (from a to b[1:] to b) by *inserting* the character b[0] at the beginning of the word b[1:], which would increment the distance by one.

Finally, you simply take the minimum edit distance of all three results (replace the first character, remove the first character, insert the first character).

This one-liner solution demonstrates once again the importance of training your recursion skills. Recursion may not come naturally to you, but rest assured that it will after studying many recursive problems like this one.

Calculating the Powerset by Using Functional Programming

In this section, you'll learn about an important mathematical concept known as the powerset: the set of all subsets. You'll need powersets in statistics, set theory, functional programming, probability theory, and algorithmic analysis.

The Basics

The *powerset* is the set of all subsets of the given set s. It includes the empty set {}, the original set s, and all other possible subsets of the original set. Here are a few examples.

Example 1:

- Given set: s = {1}
- Powerset: P = {{},{1}}

Example 2:

- Given set: s = {1, 2}
- Powerset: P = {{},{1},{2},{1,2}}

Example 3:

- Given set: s = {1, 2, 3}
- Powerset: P = {{},{1},{2},{3},{1,2},{1,3},{2,3},{1,2,3}}

To calculate a powerset P_n of a set s with n elements, you use the smaller powerset P_{n-1} of a subset of s with $(n-1)$ elements. Say you want to calculate the powerset of set $s = \{1, 2, 3\}$.

1. Initialize the powerset P_0 with zero elements as $P_0 = \{\{\}\}$. In other words, this is the powerset of the empty set. It contains only the empty set itself.

2. To create the powerset P_n with n elements from the powerset P_{n-1} with $(n-1)$ elements, you take one (arbitrary) element x from the set s and incorporate all arising subsets into the larger powerset P_n by using the following procedure:

3. Go over all sets p in P_{n-1} and create a new subset that consists of the union of x and p. This results in a new temporary set of sets T. For example, if $P_2 = \{\{\}, \{1\}, \{2\}, \{1,2\}\}$, you'll create the temporary set of sets $T = \{\{3\}, \{1,3\}, \{2,3\}, \{1,2,3\}\}$ by adding the element $x = 3$ to all sets in P_2.

4. Merge the new set of sets T with the powerset P_{n-1} to obtain powerset P_n. For example, you obtain powerset P_3 by merging the temporary set T with the powerset P_2 as follows: $P_3 = T$ union P_2.

5. Go to 2 until original set s is empty.

I'll explain this strategy in more detail in the following section.

The reduce() Function

But first, you need to properly understand an important Python function that you'll use in the one-liner: the reduce() function. The reduce() function is built into Python 2, but the developers decided it was used little enough that they didn't include it in Python 3, so you'll need to import it first from the functools library.

The reduce() function takes three arguments: reduce(function, iterable, initializer). The function arguments define how two values x and y are reduced to a single value (for example, lambda x, y: x + y). This way, you can iteratively reduce two values of an iterable (the second argument) to a single value—until only a single value is left in the iterable. The initializer argument is optional—if you don't set it, Python assumes the first value of the iterable as a default.

For example, calling reduce(lambda x, y: x + y, [0, 1, 2, 3]) performs the following computation: (((0 + 1)+ 2)+ 3) = 6. In other words, you first reduce the two values x=0 and y=1 to the sum x + y = 0 + 1 = 1. Then, you use this result of the first call of the lambda function as input to the second call of the lambda function: x=1 and y=2. The result is the sum x + y = 1 + 2 = 3. Finally, we use the result of this second call of the lambda function as input to the third call of the lambda function by setting x=3 and y=3. The result is the sum x + y = 3 + 3 = 6.

In the last example, you have seen that the value x always carries the result of the previous (lambda) function. The argument x serves as the accumulated value, while the argument y serves as the *update* value from the iterable. This is the intended behavior to iteratively "reduce" all values in the iterable argument to a single one. The optional third parameter initializer specifies the initial input for x. This allows you to define a *sequence aggregator* as shown in Listing 6-5.

List Arithmetic

Before diving into the one-liner, you need to understand two more list operators. The first is the list concatenation operator +, which glues together two lists. For example, the result of the expression [1, 2] + [3, 4] is the new list [1, 2, 3, 4]. The second is the union operator |, which performs a simple union operation on two sets. For example, the result of the expression {1, 2} | {3, 4} is the new set {1, 2, 3, 4}.

The Code

Listing 6-5 provides a one-liner solution that calculates the powerset of a given set *s*.

```
# Dependencies
from functools import reduce


# The Data
s = {1, 2, 3}


# The One-Liner
ps = lambda s: reduce(lambda P, x: ❶P + [subset | {x} for subset in P], s, ❷[set()])


# The Result
print(ps(s))
```

Listing 6-5: One-liner solution to calculate the powerset of a given set

Guess the output of this code snippet!

How It Works

The idea of this one-liner is to start the powerset as an empty set ❷ and repeatedly add subsets to it ❶ until no more subsets can be found.

Initially, the powerset contains only the empty set. In each step, you take one element x out of the data set s and create new subsets that naturally emerge by adding x to all subsets that are already in the powerset ❷. As you've seen in the introduction of this section, the size of the powerset therefore doubles each time you consider an additional element x from the data set s. In this way, you can grow the powerset with *n* subsets one data set element at a time (but by *n* subsets at a time). Note that the powerset grows exponentially: for any new data set element *x*, you double the size of the powerset. This is an inherent property of powersets: they quickly overwhelm any storage capacity—even for relatively small data sets with only a few dozen of elements.

You use the reduce() function to maintain the current powerset in the variable P (which initially contains only the empty set). Using list comprehension, the reduce() function creates new subsets—one for each existing subset—and adds them to the powerset P. In particular, it adds the value x from the data set to each subset and thus doubles the size of the powerset (containing the subsets *with* and *without* the data set element x). In this way, the reduce() function repeatedly "merges" two elements: the powerset P and an element x from the data set.

Hence, the result of the one-liner is the following:

```
# The Result
print(ps(s))
# [set(), {1}, {2}, {1, 2}, {3}, {1, 3}, {2, 3}, {1, 2, 3}]
```

This one-liner nicely demonstrates how important it is that you have a thorough understanding of lambda functions, list comprehension, and set operations.

Caesar's Cipher Encryption Using Advanced Indexing and List Comprehension

In this section, you'll learn about an ancient encryption technique called *Caesar's cipher*, used by Julius Caesar himself to obfuscate his private conversations. Unfortunately, Caesar's cipher is extremely simple to crack and offers no real protection, but it's still used for fun and obfuscation of forum content that should be protected from naive readers' eyes.

The Basics

Caesar's cipher is based on the idea of shifting characters to be encrypted by a fixed number of positions in the alphabet. We'll look at a particular case of Caesar's cipher called the ROT13 algorithm.

The *ROT13* algorithm is a simple encryption algorithm used in many forums (for example, Reddit) to prevent spoilers or hide the semantics of a conversation from newbies. The ROT13 algorithm is easy to decrypt—an attacker can crack your code by running a probabilistic analysis on the distribution of the letters in your encrypted text—even if the attacker doesn't know by how many positions you shifted each character. You should never rely on this algorithm to actually encrypt your messages! Still, there are many light applications of the ROT13 algorithm:

- Obscure the result of puzzles in online forums.

- Obscure possible spoilers for movies or books.

- Make fun of other weak encryption algorithms: "56-bit DES is at least stronger than ROT13."

- Obscure email addresses on websites against 99.999 percent of email spam bots.

So ROT13 is more of a popular running gag in internet culture and an educational tool than a serious cipher.

The algorithm can be explained in one sentence: *ROT13 = Rotate the string to be encrypted by 13 positions (modulo 26) in the alphabet of 26 characters* (see Figure 6-4).

Original, non-obfuscated letters

A	B	C	D	E	F	G	H	I	J	K	L	M	N	O	P	Q	R	S	T	U	V	W	X	Y	Z
N	O	P	Q	R	S	T	U	V	W	X	Y	Z	A	B	C	D	E	F	G	H	I	J	K	L	M

ROT13 obfuscated letters

Figure 6-4: The table shows how each character in the alphabet is encrypted and decrypted under the ROT13 algorithm.

In other words, you shift each character by 13 positions in the alphabet. When shifting over the last character, *z*, you start over at the first position in the alphabet, *a*.

The Code

Listing 6-6 creates a one-liner to encrypt the string s by using the ROT13 algorithm!

```
## Data
abc = "abcdefghijklmnopqrstuvwxyz"
s = "xthexrussiansxarexcoming"


## One-Liner
rt13 = lambda x: "".join([abc[(abc.find(c) + 13) % 26] for c in x])
```

```
## Result
print(rt13(s))
print(rt13(rt13(s)))
```

Listing 6-6: One-liner solution encrypting string s with the ROT13 algorithm

Use Figure 6-4 to crack this code: what's the output of this code snippet?

How It Works

The one-liner solution encrypts each character separately by moving it 13 positions to the right in the alphabet stored in abc, and then creates a list of these encrypted characters and joins the elements in this list to get the encrypted phrase x.

Let's take a closer look at how to encrypt each character. You use list comprehension (see Chapter 2) to create the list of encrypted characters by replacing each character c with the character 13 positions to the right in the alphabet. It's crucial to prevent overshooting for all characters in the alphabet with *index >= 13*. For instance, when shifting character z with index 25 by 13 positions, you obtain index 25 + 13 = 38, which is not a valid index of the alphabet. To fix this, you use the modulo operator to ensure that when shifting a character beyond the maximum index 25 for character z, you restart our calculation of the final position of the character to be encrypted with *index == 0* (character a). Then, you proceed shifting to the right for the remaining of the 13 positions that have not already been applied before the restart (see Figure 6-5). For example, character z is shifted by 13 positions to index 38 modulo 26 (in Python code: 38%26), which is index 12 or character m.

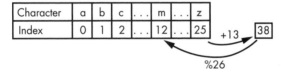

Figure 6-5: Preventing overshooting by restarting the shift operation at index 0, which results in the following shift sequence: 25 > 0 > 1 > . . . > 12

Here's the critical part of the code that shows exactly how each character c is shifted by 13 positions:

```
abc[(abc.find(c) + 13) % 26]
```

First, you find character c's index in the alphabet abc. Second, you shift the index by adding the integer 13 to character c's index in the alphabet abc considering our modulo 26 trick (as explained in the previous paragraphs).

The result of the one-liner code snippet is the following output.

```
## Result
print(rt13(s))
# kgurkehffvnafknerkpbzvat

print(rt13(rt13(s)))
# xthexrussiansxarexcoming
```

To summarize, you've learned the special variant of Caesar's cipher, the ROT13 algorithm, which shifts each character in a string by 13 positions in the alphabet. Shifting it twice by 13 + 13 = 26 index positions results in the original character, meaning encryption and decryption use the same algorithm.

Finding Prime Numbers with the Sieve of Eratosthenes

Finding prime numbers is of critical importance for practical applications such as cryptography. Many public-key methods are safe (from a cryptographic point of view) only because computation of prime factors of large numbers is generally inefficient and slow. We'll make a one-liner that uses an ancient algorithm to root out all prime numbers from a range of numbers.

The Basics

A prime number n is an integer that's not divisible without a remainder by any other integer, except for i and n. In other words, for a prime number, there are no two integers $a>1$ and $b>1$ whose product equals the prime number: $a^b=n$.

Say you want to check whether your given number n is a prime number. Let's start with a naive algorithm to determine prime numbers (see Listing 6-7).

```
def prime(n):
❶ for i in range(2,n):
    ❷ if n % i == 0:
            return False
    return True


print(prime(10))
# False

print(prime(11))
# True

print(prime(7919))
# True
```

Listing 6-7: Naive implementation to check whether a given number n is prime

The algorithm checks all numbers between 2 and n-1 ❶ to see whether the number n will divide evenly into it with no remainders ❷. For example, when determining whether number n = 10 is a prime number, the algorithm quickly realizes that the expression n % i == 0 evaluates to True for i = 2. It has found a number i that is a divisor of n, so n cannot be a prime number. In this case, the algorithm aborts any further computation and returns False.

The time complexity for checking a single number is the same as the input n: in the worst case, the algorithm needs n loop iterations to check whether number n is a prime number.

Say you want to calculate all prime numbers from 2 to a certain maximal number m. You could simply repeat the prime test from Listing 6-7 m-1 times (see Listing 6-8). However, this comes at huge processing cost.

```
# Find all prime numbers <= m
m = 20
primes = [n for n in range(2,m+1) if prime(n)]

print(primes)
# [2, 3, 5, 7, 11, 13, 17, 19]
```

Listing 6-8: Finding all prime numbers up to a maximal number m

Here we use list comprehension (see Chapter 2) to create a list with all prime numbers smaller than m. We introduce a for loop, meaning the algorithm requires m function calls of is_prime(n) and so the time complexity is bounded by m**2. The number of operations grows quadratically with the input m. To find all prime numbers smaller than m = 100 takes up to m**2 = 10000 operations!

We'll build a one-liner to drastically reduce this time cost.

The Code

With this one-liner, we'll write an algorithm to find all prime numbers up to a maximal integer number m that is more time efficient than our naive implementation. The one-liner in Listing 6-9 is inspired by an ancient algorithm called the Sieve of Eratosthenes, which I'll explain in this section.

```
## Dependencies
from functools import reduce

## The Data
n=100

## The One-Liner
primes = reduce(lambda r, x: r - set(range(x**2, n, x)) if x in r else r,
                range(2, int(n**0.5) + 1), set(range(2, n)))
## The Result
print(primes)
# {2, 3, 5, 7, 11, 13, 17, 19, 23, 29, 31, 37, 41, 43,
#  47, 53, 59, 61, 67, 71, 73, 79, 83, 89, 97}
```

Listing 6-9: One-liner solution implementing the Sieve of Eratosthenes

You'll likely need some additional background knowledge to understand what happens here.

How It Works

To be frank, I was hesitant to include this one-liner in the book. It's confusing, complex, and unreadable. Still, this is the type of code you face in practice, and with this book, I want to ensure you're able to understand every single line of code—even if it takes some time. I stumbled upon a version of this one-liner at StackOverflow. It is loosely based on an ancient algorithm called the *Sieve of Eratosthenes* that was designed to calculate prime numbers.

NOTE *I modified the original StackOverflow one-liner for clarity. The original one-liner can be found at* https://stackoverflow.com/questions/10639861/python-prime -generator-in-one-line/ *at the time of this writing.*

The Sieve of Eratosthenes Algorithm

The algorithm creates (conceptually) a huge array of numbers from 2 to m, the maximal integer number. All the numbers in the array are *prime candidates*, which means that the algorithm considers them to be prime numbers *potentially* (but not *necessarily*). During the algorithm, you sieve out the candidates that cannot be prime. Only the ones that remain after this filtering process are the final prime numbers.

To accomplish this, the algorithm calculates and marks the numbers in this array that are not prime numbers. At the end, all unmarked numbers are prime numbers.

The algorithm repeats the following steps:

1. Start with the first number 2 and increment it in every step of the process until you find a prime number x. You know that x is prime if it is unmarked because the fact that x is unmarked means that no smaller number than x is a divisor of x—the definition of a prime number.

2. Mark all multiples of number x because they are also not prime: number x is a divisor of all those numbers.

3. Perform simple optimization: start marking multiples from number x × x instead of $2x$ because all numbers between $2x$ and x × x are already marked. There is a simple mathematical argument for this that I will describe later. For now, know that you can start marking from x × x.

Figures 6-6 to 6-11 explain this algorithm step-by-step.

Start

1	2	3	4	5	6	7	8	9	10
11	12	13	14	15	16	17	18	19	20
21	22	23	24	25	26	27	28	29	30
31	32	33	34	35	36	37	38	39	40
41	42	43	44	45	46	47	48	49	50
51	52	53	54	55	56	57	58	59	60
61	62	63	64	65	66	67	68	69	70
71	72	73	74	75	76	77	78	79	80
81	82	83	84	85	86	87	88	89	90
91	92	93	94	95	96	97	98	99	100

Figure 6-6: Initializing the Sieve of Eratosthenes algorithm

Initially, all numbers between 2 and $m = 100$ are unmarked (white cells). The first unmarked number 2 is a prime number.

Is Prime — Mark all multiples of 2

1	2	3	4	5	6	7	8	9	10
11	12	13	14	15	16	17	18	19	20
21	22	23	24	25	26	27	28	29	30
31	32	33	34	35	36	37	38	39	40
41	42	43	44	45	46	47	48	49	50
51	52	53	54	55	56	57	58	59	60
61	62	63	64	65	66	67	68	69	70
71	72	73	74	75	76	77	78	79	80
81	82	83	84	85	86	87	88	89	90
91	92	93	94	95	96	97	98	99	100

Figure 6-7: Mark all multiples of 2 because they are not prime. Ignore the marked numbers for the rest of the algorithm.

Is Prime   Mark all multiples of 3 (Start from 3²)

1	2	3	4	5	6	7	8	9	10
11	12	13	14	15	16	17	18	19	20
21	22	23	24	25	26	27	28	29	30
31	32	33	34	35	36	37	38	39	40
41	42	43	44	45	46	47	48	49	50
51	52	53	54	55	56	57	58	59	60
61	62	63	64	65	66	67	68	69	70
71	72	73	74	75	76	77	78	79	80
81	82	83	84	85	86	87	88	89	90
91	92	93	94	95	96	97	98	99	100

Figure 6-8: Mark multiples of 3 as "non-prime."

Increment to the next unmarked number, 3. Because it is unmarked at this point, it is a prime number. Because you have marked all multiples of numbers smaller than the current number 3, no smaller number is a divisor of 3. By definition, number 3 must be prime. Mark all multiples of 3 because they are not prime. Start marking from number 3 × 3 because all multiples of 3 between 3 and 3 × 3 = 9 are already marked.

Is Prime   Mark all multiples of 5 (Start from 5²)

1	2	3	4	5	6	7	8	9	10
11	12	13	14	15	16	17	18	19	20
21	22	23	24	25	26	27	28	29	30
31	32	33	34	35	36	37	38	39	40
41	42	43	44	45	46	47	48	49	50
51	52	53	54	55	56	57	58	59	60
61	62	63	64	65	66	67	68	69	70
71	72	73	74	75	76	77	78	79	80
81	82	83	84	85	86	87	88	89	90
91	92	93	94	95	96	97	98	99	100

Figure 6-9: Mark multiples of 5 as "non-prime."

Go to the next unmarked number, 5 (which is a prime number). Mark all multiples of 5. Start marking from number 5 × 5 because all multiples of 5 between 5 and 5 × 5 = 25 are already marked.

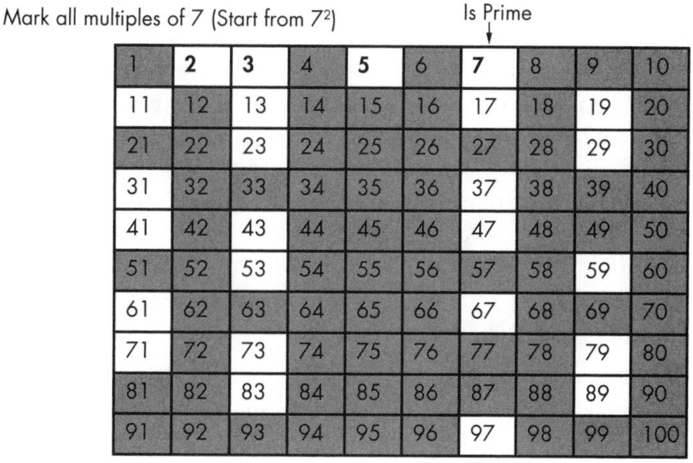

Mark all multiples of 7 (Start from 7²)   Is Prime ↓

1	2	3	4	5	6	7	8	9	10
11	12	13	14	15	16	17	18	19	20
21	22	23	24	25	26	27	28	29	30
31	32	33	34	35	36	37	38	39	40
41	42	43	44	45	46	47	48	49	50
51	52	53	54	55	56	57	58	59	60
61	62	63	64	65	66	67	68	69	70
71	72	73	74	75	76	77	78	79	80
81	82	83	84	85	86	87	88	89	90
91	92	93	94	95	96	97	98	99	100

Figure 6-10: Mark multiples of 7 as "non-prime."

Increment to the next unmarked number, 7 (which is a prime number). Mark all multiples of 7. Start marking from number 7×7 because all multiples of 7 between 7 and $7 \times 7 = 49$ are already marked.

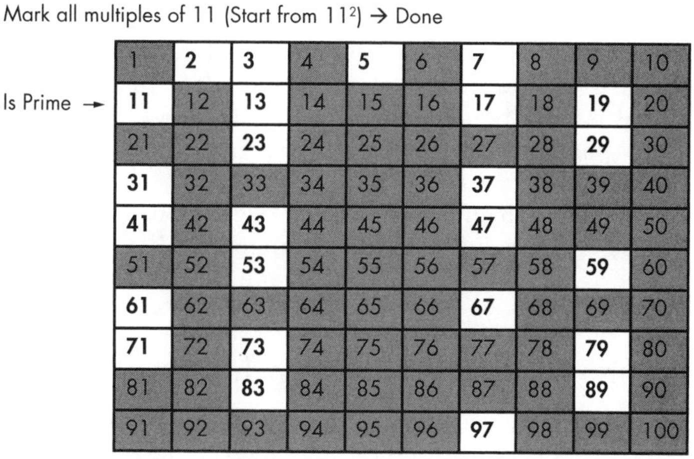

Mark all multiples of 11 (Start from 11²) → Done

Is Prime →

1	2	3	4	5	6	7	8	9	10
11	12	13	14	15	16	17	18	19	20
21	22	23	24	25	26	27	28	29	30
31	32	33	34	35	36	37	38	39	40
41	42	43	44	45	46	47	48	49	50
51	52	53	54	55	56	57	58	59	60
61	62	63	64	65	66	67	68	69	70
71	72	73	74	75	76	77	78	79	80
81	82	83	84	85	86	87	88	89	90
91	92	93	94	95	96	97	98	99	100

Figure 6-11: Mark multiples of 11 as "non-prime."

Increment to the next unmarked number, 11 (which is a prime number). Mark all multiples of 11. Because you would start marking from number $11 \times 11 = 121$, you realize that this is already larger than our maximal number $m = 100$. This causes the algorithm to terminate. All remaining unmarked numbers are not divisible by any number and are, therefore, prime numbers.

The Sieve of Eratosthenes is much more efficient than the naive algorithm because the naive algorithm checks each number *independently*, ignoring all previous computations. The Sieve of Eratosthenes, on the other hand, *reuses* results from previous computational steps—a common idea in many areas of algorithmic optimization. Each time we cross out multiples of a prime number, we essentially save ourselves the tedious work of checking whether this multiple is a prime number: we already know that it isn't.

You may wonder why we start marking from the squared prime number instead of the prime number itself. For example, in the algorithm in Figure 6-10, you just found prime number 7 and start marking from number $7 \times 7 = 49$. The reason is that you already marked all other multiples in previous iterations $7 \times 2, 7 \times 3, 7 \times 4, 7 \times 5, 7 \times 6$ because you marked all multiples of numbers smaller than the current prime number 7: 2, 3, 4, 5, 6.

One-Liner Explained

Equipped with a thorough conceptual understanding of the algorithm, you can now start investigating the one-liner solution:

```
## The One-Liner
primes = reduce(lambda r, x: r - set(range(x**2, n, x)) if x in r else r,
                range(2, int(n**0.5) + 1), set(range(2, n)))
```

This one-liner uses the reduce() function to remove, one step at a time, all marked numbers from the initial set of all numbers between 2 and n (in the one-liner: set(range(2, n))).

You take this set as the initial value for the set of unmarked values r because, initially, all values are unmarked. Now the one-liner goes over all numbers x between 2 and the square root of n (in the one-liner: range(2, int(n**0.5) + 1)) and removes the multiples of x from the set r (starting at x**2)—but only if the number x is a prime number, known because it is not removed from the set r at the current time.

Spend 5–15 minutes rereading this explanation and study the different parts of the one-liner carefully. I promise you'll find this exercise worthwhile, as it will significantly improve your Python code understanding skills.

Calculating the Fibonacci Series with the reduce() Function

The popular Italian mathematician Fibonacci (original name: Leonardo of Pisa) introduced the Fibonacci numbers in the year 1202 with the surprising observation that these numbers have significance in fields as various as math, art, and biology. This section will show you how to compute the Fibonacci numbers in a single line of code.

The Basics

The Fibonacci series starts with the numbers 0 and 1, and then, each element that follows is the sum of the two previous series elements. The Fibonacci series has the algorithm built in!

The Code

Listing 6-10 calculates a list of the *n* first Fibonacci numbers starting with the numbers 0 and 1.

```
# Dependencies
from functools import reduce


# The Data
n = 10


# The One-Liner
fibs = reduce(lambda x, _: x + [x[-2] + x[-1]], [0] * (n-2), [0, 1])


# The Result
print(fibs)
```

Listing 6-10: Calculating the Fibonacci series in one line of Python code

Study this code and take a guess at the output.

How It Works

You'll again use the powerful reduce() function. In general, this function is useful if you want to aggregate state information that's computed on the fly; for example, when you use the previous two Fibonacci numbers just computed to compute the next Fibonacci number. This is difficult to achieve with list comprehension (see Chapter 2), which can't generally access the values that have been newly created from the list comprehension.

You use the reduce() function with three arguments that correspond to reduce(function, iterable, initializer) to consecutively add the new Fibonacci number to an aggregator object that incorporates one value at a time from the iterable object as specified by the function.

Here, you use a simple list as the aggregator object with the two initial Fibonacci numbers [0, 1]. Remember that the aggregator object is handed as the first argument to the function (in our example, x).

The second argument is the next element from the iterable. However, you initialized the iterable with (n-2) dummy values in order to force the reduce() function to execute function (n-2) times (the goal is to find the first n Fibonacci numbers—but you already have the first two, 0 and 1) You use the throwaway parameter _ to indicate that you are not interested in the dummy values of the iterable. Instead, you simply append the new Fibonacci number to the aggregator list x, calculated as the sum of the previous two Fibonacci numbers.

AN ALTERNATIVE MULTILINE SOLUTION

Repeatedly summing two Fibonacci numbers was already the simple idea of the one-liner in Listing 6-10. Listing 6-11 gives a beautiful alternative solution.

```
n = 10
x = [0,1]
fibs = x[0:2] + [x.append(x[-1] + x[-2]) or x[-1] for i in range(n-2)]
print(fibs)
# [0, 1, 1, 2, 3, 5, 8, 13, 21, 34]
```

Listing 6-11: One-liner solution to find the Fibonacci numbers in an iterative manner

This code snippet was submitted by one of my email subscribers (feel free to join us at *https://blog.finxter.com/subscribe/*) and uses list comprehension with side effects: the variable x is updated n-2 times with the new Fibonacci series element. Note that the append() function has no return value, but returns None, which evaluates to False. Thus, the list comprehension statement generates a list of integers using the following idea:

```
print(0 or 10)
# 10
```

It doesn't seem correct to perform the or operation on two integers, but remember that the Boolean type is based on the integer type. Every integer value other than 0 is interpreted as True. Thus, the or operation simply uses the second integer value as a return value instead of converting it to an explicit Boolean value of True. A fine piece of Python code!

In summary, you've improved your understanding of another important pattern for Python one-liners: using the reduce() function to create a list that dynamically uses the freshly updated or added list elements to compute new list elements. You will find this useful pattern quite often in practice.

A Recursive Binary Search Algorithm

In this section, you'll learn about a basic algorithm every computer scientist must know: the binary search algorithm. Binary search has important practical applications in many implementations of basic data structures such as sets, trees, dictionaries, hash sets, hash tables, maps, and arrays. You use these data structures in every single nontrivial program.

The Basics

In brief, the *binary search algorithm* searches a sorted sequence of values 1 for a particular value x by repeatedly reducing the size of the sequence by half until only a single value is left: either it's the searched value or it doesn't exist in the sequence. In the following, you will examine this general idea in detail.

For example, say you want to search a sorted list for value 56. A naive algorithm would start with the first list element, check whether it's equal to the value 56, and move on to the next list element until it has checked all elements or found its value. In the worst case, the algorithm goes over every list element. A sorted list with 10,000 elements would take approximately 10,000 operations to check each list element for equality with the searched value. In algorithmic theory language, we say that the runtime complexity is *linear* in the number of list elements. The algorithm does not leverage all the available information to achieve the greatest efficiency.

The first piece of useful information is that the list is sorted! Using this fact, you can create an algorithm that touches only a few elements in the list and still knows with absolute certainty whether an element exists in the list. The binary search algorithm traverses only *log2(n)* elements (logarithm of base 2). You can search the same list of 10,000 elements by using only *log2*(10,000) < 14 operations!

For a binary search, you assume the list is sorted in an ascending manner. The algorithm starts by checking the middle element. If the middle value is bigger than the value you want, you know that all elements between the middle and the last list elements are larger than the value you want. The value you want won't exist in this half of the list, so you can immediately reject half of the list elements with a single operation.

Similarly, if the searched value is larger than the middle element, you can reject the first half of the list elements. You then simply repeat the procedure of halving the effective list size of elements to be checked in each step of the algorithm. Figure 6-12 shows a visual example.

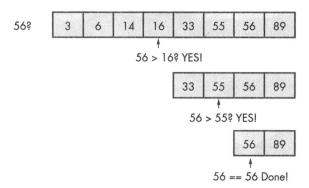

Figure 6-12: Example run of the binary search algorithm

If the sublist contains an even number of elements, there's no obvious middle element. In this case, you round down the index of the middle element.

You want to find the value 56 in the sorted list of eight integer values while touching as few elements as possible. The binary search algorithm checks middle element *x* (rounding down), then discards the half of the list that 56 cannot possibly be in. There are three general results of this check:

- Element *x* is larger than 56. The algorithm ignores the right part of the list.

- Element *x* is smaller than value 56. The algorithm ignores the left part of the list.

- Element *x* is equal to value 56, as in the last line in Figure 6-12. Congratulations—you have just found desired value!

Listing 6-12 shows a practical implementation of the binary search algorithm.

```
def binary_search(lst, value):
    lo, hi = 0, len(lst)-1
    while lo <= hi:
        mid = (lo + hi) // 2
        if lst[mid] < value:
            lo = mid + 1
        elif value < lst[mid]:
            hi = mid - 1
        else:
            return mid
    return -1


l = [3, 6, 14, 16, 33, 55, 56, 89]
x = 56
print(binary_search(l,x))
# 6 (the index of the found element)
```

Listing 6-12: The binary search algorithm

This algorithm takes as arguments a list and a value to search for. It then repeatedly halves the search space by using the two variables lo and hi, which define the interval of possible list elements in which the desired value could exist: lo defines the start index, and hi defines the end index of the interval. You check which of the cases the mid element falls in and adapt the interval of potential elements accordingly by modifying the lo and hi values as described.

While this is a perfectly valid, readable, and efficient implementation of the binary search algorithm, it's not a one-liner solution, yet!

The Code

Now you'll implement the binary search algorithm in a single line of code (see Listing 6-13)!

```
## The Data
l = [3, 6, 14, 16, 33, 55, 56, 89]
x = 33

## The One-Liner
❶ bs = lambda l, x, lo, hi: -1 if lo>hi else \
     ❷ (lo+hi)//2 if l[(lo+hi)//2] == x else \
     ❸ bs(l, x, lo, (lo+hi)//2-1) if l[(lo+hi)//2] > x else \
     ❹ bs(l, x, (lo+hi)//2+1, hi)


## The Results
print(bs(l, x, 0, len(l)-1))
```

Listing 6-13: One-liner solution to implement binary search

Guess the output of this code snippet!

How It Works

Because binary search lends itself naturally to a recursive approach, studying this one-liner will strengthen your intuitive understanding of this important computer science concept. Note that I've broken this one-liner solution into four lines for readability, though you can, of course, write it in a single line of code. In this one-liner, I've used a recursive way of defining the binary search algorithm.

You create a new function bs by using the lambda operator with four arguments: l, x, lo, and hi ❶. The first two arguments l and x are variables with the sorted list and the value to search for. The lo and hi arguments define the minimal and the maximal index of the current sublist to be searched for the value x. At each recursion level, the code checks a sublist specified by the indices hi and lo, which becomes smaller and smaller by increasing the index lo and decreasing the index hi. After a finite number of steps, the condition lo>hi holds True. The searched sublist is empty— and you haven't found the value x. This is the base case of our recursion. Because you haven't found element x, you return -1, indicating that no such element exists.

You use the calculation (lo+hi)//2 to find the middle element of the sublist. If this happens to be your desired value, you return the index of that mid element ❷. Note that you use integer division to round down to the next integer value that can be used as a list index.

If the mid element is larger than the desired value, it means the elements on the right are also larger, so you call the function recursively but adapt the hi index to consider only list elements on the left of the mid element ❸.

Similarly, if the mid element is smaller than the desired value, there is no need to search all elements on the left of the mid element, so you call the function recursively but adapt the lo index to consider only list elements on the right of the mid element ❹.

When searching for the value 33 in the list [3, 6, 14, 16, 33, 55, 56, 89], the result is the index 4.

This one-liner section has strengthened your general code understanding regarding features such as conditional execution, basic keywords, and arithmetic operations, as well as the important topic of programmatic sequence indexing. More important, you've learned how to use recursion to make complex problems easier.

A Recursive Quicksort Algorithm

Now you'll build a one-liner to use the popular algorithm *Quicksort*, a sorting algorithm that, as the name suggests, quickly sorts the data.

The Basics

Quicksort is both a popular question in many code interviews (asked by Google, Facebook, and Amazon) and a practical sorting algorithm that's fast, concise, and readable. Because of its elegance, most introductory algorithm classes cover Quicksort.

Quicksort sorts a list by recursively dividing the big problem into smaller problems and combining the solutions from the smaller problems in a way that it solves the big problem.

To solve each smaller problem, the same strategy is used recursively: the smaller problems are divided into even smaller subproblems, solved separately, and combined, placing Quicksort in the class of *Divide and Conquer* algorithms.

Quicksort selects a *pivot* element and then places all elements that are larger than the pivot to the right, and all elements that are smaller than or equal to the pivot to the left. This divides the big problem of sorting the list into two smaller subproblems: sorting two smaller lists. You then repeat this procedure recursively until you obtain a list with zero elements that, being sorted, causes the recursion to terminate.

Figure 6-13 shows the Quicksort algorithm in action.

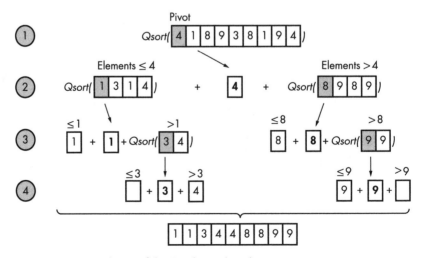

Figure 6-13: Example run of the Quicksort algorithm

Figure 6-13 shows the Quicksort algorithm on a list of unsorted integers [4, 1, 8, 9, 3, 8, 1, 9, 4]. First, it selects 4 as the pivot element, splits up the list into an unsorted sublist [1, 3, 1, 4] with all elements that are smaller than or equal to the pivot, and an unsorted sublist [8, 9, 8, 9] with all elements that are larger than the pivot.

Next, the Quicksort algorithm is called recursively on the two unsorted sublists to sort them. As soon as the sublists contain maximally one element, they are sorted by definition, and the recursion ends.

At every recursion level, the three sublists (left, pivot, right) are concatenated before the resulting list is handed to the higher recursion level.

The Code

You'll create a function q that implements the Quicksort algorithm in a single line of Python and sorts any argument given as a list of integers (see Listing 6-14).

```
## The Data
unsorted = [33, 2, 3, 45, 6, 54, 33]


## The One-Liner
q = lambda l: q([x for x in l[1:] if x <= l[0]]) + [l[0]] + q([x for x in l if x > l[0]]) if l else []


## The Result
print(q(unsorted))
```

Listing 6-14: One-liner solution for the Quicksort algorithm using recursion

Now, can you guess—one last time—the output of the code?

How It Works

The one-liner directly resembles the algorithm we just discussed. First, you create a new lambda function q that takes one list argument l to sort. From a high-level perspective, the lambda function has the following basic structure:

```
lambda l: q(left) + pivot + q(right) if l else []
```

In the recursion base case—that is, the case that the list is empty and, therefore, trivially sorted—the lambda function returns the empty list [].

In any other case, the function selects the pivot element as the first element of list l, and divides all elements into two sublists (left and right) based on whether they are smaller or larger than the pivot. To achieve this, you use simple list comprehension (see Chapter 2). As the two sublists are not necessarily sorted, you recursively execute the Quicksort algorithm on them too. Finally, you combine all three lists and return the sorted list. Therefore, the result is as follows:

```
## The Result
print(q(unsorted))
# [2, 3, 6, 33, 33, 45, 54]
```

Summary

In this chapter, you've learned important algorithms in computer science addressing a wide range of topics including anagrams, palindromes, power-sets, permutations, factorials, prime numbers, Fibonacci numbers, obfuscation, searching, and sorting. Many of these form the basis of more advanced algorithms and contain the seeds of a thorough algorithmic education. Advancing your knowledge of algorithms and algorithmic theory is one of the most effective ways to improve as a coder. I would even say that the lack of algorithmic understanding is the number one reason most intermediate coders feel stuck in their learning progress.

To help you get unstuck, I regularly explain new algorithms in my "Coffee Break Python" email series for continuous improvement (visit *https://blog.finxter.com/subscribe/*). I appreciate you spending your valuable time and effort studying all the one-liner code snippets and explanations, and I hope you can already see how your skills have improved. Based on my experience teaching thousands of Python learners, more than half the intermediate coders struggle with understanding basic Python one-liners. With commitment and persistence, you have a good chance of leaving the intermediate coders behind and becoming a Python master (or at least a top 10 percent coder).

AFTERWORD

Congratulations! You've worked through this whole book and mastered the *Python one-liner* like only a few people ever will. You have built yourself a strong foundation that will help you break through the ceiling of your Python coding skills. By carefully working through all the Python one-liners, you should be able to conquer any single line of Python code you will ever face.

As with any superpower, you must use it wisely. Misuse of one-liners will harm your code projects. In this book, I compressed all algorithms into a single line of code with the purpose of pushing your code understanding skills to the next level. But you should be careful not to *overuse* your skill in your practical code projects. Don't cram everything into a single line of code just to show off your one-liner superpower.

Instead, why not use it to make existing codebases more readable by unraveling their most complex one-liners? Much like Superman uses his superpowers to help normal people live their comfortable lives, you can help normal coders maintain their comfortable programmer lives.

This book's main promise was to make you a master of Python one-liners. If you feel that the book delivered on this promise, please give it a vote on your favorite book marketplace (such as Amazon) to help others discover it. I also encourage you to leave me a note at *chris@finxter.com* if you encountered any problem with the book, or wish to provide any positive or negative feedback. We would love to improve the book continuously, considering your feedback in future editions, so I'll give away a free copy of my *Coffee Break Python Slicing* ebook to anyone who writes in with constructive feedback.

Finally, if you seek continuous improvement of your own Python skills, subscribe to my Python newsletter at *https://blog.finxter.com/subscribe/*, where I release new educational computer science content such as Python cheat sheets almost daily to offer you—and thousands of other ambitious coders—a clear path to continuous improvement and, ultimately, mastery in Python.

Now that you've mastered the single line of code, you should consider shifting your focus to larger code projects. Learn about object-oriented programming and project management, and, most importantly, choose your own practical code projects to constantly work on. This improves your learning retention, is highly motivating and encouraging, creates value in the real world, and is the most realistic form of training. Nothing can replace practical experience in terms of learning efficiency.

I encourage my students to spend at least 70 percent of their learning time working on practical projects. If you have 100 minutes each day for learning, spend 70 minutes working on a practical code project and only 30 minutes reading books and working through courses and tutorials. This seems obvious, but most people still do this wrong and so never feel quite ready to start working on practical code projects.

It has been a pleasure to spend such a long time with you, and I highly appreciate the time you invested in this training book. May your investment turn out to be a profitable one! I wish you all the best for your coding career and hope that we'll meet again.

Happy coding!
Chris

INDEX

index() list method, 8
inference phase, 83
initializer argument, 163–164
in keyword, 5, 11, 25
insert() list method, 7
Instagram influencer filtering
example, 57–59
instances ({}) regex operator, 134,
135, 142
integer data type and operations, 2, 50
integer division (//) operator, 2
int() function, 2
investment portfolio risk example,
114–116
is keyword, 6
items() dictionary method, 11, 20
iterable arguments, 34
iterable (reduce()) argument,
163–164, 175

J

join() string method, 5, 166

K

(key, value) pairs, 10–11
keys() function, 11
K-Means algorithm, 95–99
KMeans module, 97–99
K-Nearest Neighbors (KNN) algorithm,
100–104
KNeighborsClassifier module, 103
KNeighborsRegressor module, 101–103

L

labeled vs. unlabeled data, 94–95
lambda functions
defining, 15–16, 24–26
recursive, 158–159, 160–162
lambda keyword, 15
len() function, 6
len() string method, 5
Levenshtein distance algorithm,
159–162
linear classifiers, 120
linear regression, 83–89
coding, 86–89
concepts and formulas, 83–86
LinearRegression module, 87

list comprehension
examples, 22–24, 115, 139
formula, 12, 18–20
and generator expressions, 36
nested, 21–22
with slicing, 29–30
lists. *See also* list comprehension
concatenation, 7, 33–35, 162–165
defining, 6
membership testing, 11
vs. NumPy arrays, 42, 43
operations on, 6–8
logical_and() function, 72–74
logistic regression, 89–94
LogisticRegression module, 92–93
loops, 13–14
lower() string method, 4
lung cancer logistic regression
example, 90–94

M

machine learning
bias-variance trade-off, 113–114
classification concepts, 120
decision trees, 111–113
ensemble learning, 123–126
K-Means clustering algorithm,
94–99
K-Nearest Neighbors algorithm,
100–104
linear regression algorithm, 83–89
logistic regression algorithm,
89–94
model parameters, 83
neural network analysis, 104–110
overview, 81, 126
supervised, 82–83
support-vector machines, 119,
121–123
unsupervised, 94–95
machine learning models
decision trees, 111–113
K-Means clustering algorithm,
94–99
K-Nearest Neighbors algorithm,
100–104
linear regression function, 83–89
logistic regression function, 89–94
neural networks, 104–110
parameters, 83

random forests, 123–126
support-vector machines, 119,
121–123
map() function, 25–26
margin of error, 121
margin of safety, 123
mark non-prime numbers example,
169–174
mark string example, 25–26
mask index arrays, 59
match() function, 133–134, 135–136
Matplotlib library, 34, 71–72
max() function, 44–45, 46, 79
maximum likelihood models, 91–92
max_iter() argument, 109
mean, 70–71, 73–74
mean() function, 73
meta-predictions, 123
min() function, 44, 115
minimum wage test example, 35–37
MLPRegressor module, 108–110
modulo (%) operator, 2, 167
multilayer perceptron (MLP), 104–110
multiline strings, 4, 130, 137, 140–141,
149–150
multinomial classification, 90
multiplication of arrays, 45, 50, 73
multiplication (*) operator, 2, 43, 45, 50
multiset data structures, 10
mutability, 6–7

N

named groups, 145–147
n_clusters argument, 98
ndim attribute, 48–49
negation (-) operator, 2
negative lookahead, 149–150
negative lookahead (?!) regex
operator, 149
n_estimators parameter, 124–125
neural network analysis
coding, 108–110
concepts of artificial, 106–107
example, 104–105
newline (\n) character, 4, 22, 23, 130
None keyword, 4, 5–6
nongreedy asterisk (*) regex operator,
130–131, 134
nongreedy pattern matching, 130–131,
134, 137
nonlinear classifiers, 120

nonsecure URL search example,
140–141
nonzero() function, 54–56
normal distribution data, 70–71
normal() function, 71
not keyword, 3–4
not (^) regex operator, 140, 145–147
null value. *See* None keyword
numerical data types and operations, 2
NumPy arrays
arithmetic operations on, 43–46, 72
axes and dimensionality, 48–50
axis argument, 61–63, 65–66, 76
Boolean operations, 54–56
broadcasting, 50, 52–53, 54–56
creating, 42–43
and data types, 50–51, 53, 59
filtering, 68–69
indexing, 46, 57–59
logical and operation, 72–73
minimum variance calculation,
114–116
reshaping, 61, 62–63
slice assignments, 60–61, 62–63
slicing, 46–48, 51–52, 58–59,
75–76, 78
sorting in, 64–67
statistics calculations, 116–119
NumPy library, 41, 43

O

obfuscation algorithm, 165–168
one-liners
resources, xxiii
use and misuse, 183–184
value of learning, xix–xxii
or keyword, 3–4
order of execution
in Boolean operations, 3–4
in regular expressions, 135
or (|) regex operator, 135, 144
outlier detection, 53–57, 70, 73–74

P

palindrome detection example, 154–156
pattern matching. *See* regular expressions
permutations calculation example,
156–159
Peters, Tim, *The Zen of Python*, xxi–xxii
pivot element, 180–183

plot() function, 34–35
pop() list method, 9
power (**) operator, 2
powersets, 162–165
predict() function, 88, 108–110,
    122, 125
predictions and features, 82–83
predict_proba() function, 93–94
prime numbers
    detection example, 168–169
    generator example, 169–174
probability, a priori, 157
programming skills
    and algorithm mastery, 151–152
    development and practice, xix–xxii,
        116, 126, 183–184
    problem solving strategies, 143
    productivity, 39–40, 87, 127
    in rating example, 104–105,
        109–110
pruning, 112
Python
    code readability, xxi–xxii, 24, 116
    libraries, xix–xx, 26, 41, 71, 86,
        87, 163
    naming conventions, 98
    object truth values, 160–161
    resources, xxiii
    skills rating example, 104–105,
        109–110

Q

Quicksort algorithm, 180–182
quotes
    in regex expressions, 145, 145–150
    in strings, 4

R

RandomForestClassifier module, 124
random forests, 123–126
random module, 71
randomness in decision trees, 113,
    125–126
random_state parameter, 125
range() function, 12, 18–20, 169, 174
reading files example, 22–24
recursion and recursive functions,
    157–159, 160–162, 177–180,
    180–182
reduce() function, 163–165, 169, 174,
    175–176

regex. *See* regular expressions
regex characters, 128–131, 134–135,
    138, 140–141
regex functions, 135, 137, 142–143, 149
regression problems
    vs. classification problems, 89
    and K-Nearest Neighbors
        algorithm, 100–101
    and linear regression algorithm, 83
regular expressions. *See also* regex
        characters; regex functions
    for character substitution, 149–150
    compiled patterns, 133–134
    for duplicate character detection,
        145–147
    false positives removal, 132–134
    greedy and non-greedy pattern
        matching, 130
    groups and named groups, 138–
        139, 145–146
    negative lookahead, 149–150
    special characters, 138
    for user input validation, 141–145
    for word repetition detection,
        147–148
re module, 129–131
remove() list method, 7–8
replace() string method, 5
replication (*) operator, 34–35
reshape() function, 62–63, 88, 92–93,
    101–103
return expressions, 15, 24–25
return keyword, 15
return values, 6, 24
reverse() list method, 8
ROT13 algorithm, 165–168

S

salary increase calculation example,
    51–53
SAT score analysis example, 66–67
scikit-learn library, 86, 97–98
search() function, 135, 147
sequence aggregator examples,
    164–165, 175
set comprehension, 12
sets
    data structure, 9–10, 56
    membership testing, 11–12
    powerset construction example,
        162–165

shape attribute, 49–50, 76
Sieve of Eratosthenes, 169–174
sigmoid function, 90–92
single quote ('), 4
sklearn package, 98
slice assignments, 31–33, 60–61
slicing
    with list comprehension, 29–30
    multidimensional, 46–48
    with negative step size, 66, 67,
        155–156
    syntax and examples, 26–29
softmax function, 90
sorted (Python) function, 65, 66,
    153–154
sort() (NumPy) function, 64–66, 67
sorting, 64–67, 153–154, 180–182
sort() list method, 8
split() function, 21–22
Stack Overflow, 170
stacks, 8–9
standard deviation, 70–71, 73–74, 117
start argument, 27, 155
startswith() string method, 5
statistics calculations, 116–119
std() function, 73, 117–119
step argument, 27
stock price examples
    calculations, 61–62
    linear regression, 84–89
stop argument, 27, 155
strings. *See also* multiline strings;
        regular expressions
    data type, 4
    selected methods, 4–5
strip() string method, 4, 22–24
str() string method, 4
sub() regex function, 149–150
subtraction (-) operator, 2, 43, 45
sum() function, 76, 77, 78
supervised machine learning, 82–83, 94
support-vector classification (SVC), 122
support-vector machines (SVMs), 119,
    121–123
SVC module, 122

T

tab (\t) character, 4
team rankings example, 156–157
throwaway (_) parameter, 175

time format validation examples,
    141–145
trailing underscore (_) character, 98
training data, 82–83, 100
tree module, 112–113
trees. *See* decision trees
triple quote ('''), 4
True value. *See also* Boolean data
    of Python objects, 160–161
    and while loops, 14

U

union (|) operator, 164–165
unlabeled vs. labeled data, 94–95
unpacking (*) operator, 38
unsupervised machine learning, 94–95
upper() string method, 5
urllib.request module, 132
urlopen() method, 132
URL search example, 140–141
user input validation examples, 141–145

V

values() function, 11, 36–37
van Rossum, Guido, 36
var() function, 115, 117–119
variance, 113–116, 126

W

web scraper example, 132–134
where() function, 116
while loops, 13–14
whitespace (\s) character, 4, 145–148
word repetition detection example,
    147–148

X

xkcd() function, 71–72

Z

Zen of Python, The (Peters), xxi–xxii
zero-or-one (?) regex operator, 130,
    134, 139
zip() function, 37–39